KU-605-188

Collins
French
phrasebook

Consultant
Sophie Karnavos

First published 1993
This edition published 2007
Copyright © HarperCollins Publishers
Reprint 10 9 8 7 6 5 4 3 2
Typeset by Davidson Pre-Press, Glasgow
Printed in Malaysia by Imago

www.collinslanguage.com

ISBN 978-0-00-724668-7

Using your phrasebook

Your *Collins Gem Phrasebook* is designed to help you locate the exact phrase you need, when you need it, whether on holiday or for business. If you want to adapt the phrases, you can easily see where to substitute your own words using the dictionary section, and the clear, full-colour layout gives you direct access to the different topics.

The Gem Phrasebook includes:

- Over 70 topics arranged thematically. Each phrase is accompanied by a simple pronunciation guide which eliminates any problems pronouncing foreign words.

- A Top ten tips section to safeguard against any cultural faux pas, giving essential dos and don'ts for situations involving local customs or etiquette.

- Practical hints to make your stay trouble free, showing you where to go and what to do when dealing with everyday matters such as travel or hotels and offering valuable tourist information.

- Face to face sections so that you understand what it is being said to you. These example mini-dialogues give you a good idea of what to expect from a real conversation.

- Common announcements and messages you may hear, ensuring that you never miss the important information you need to know when out and about.

- A clearly laid-out 3000-word dictionary means you will never be stuck for words.

- A basic grammar section which will enable you to build on your phrases.

- A list of public holidays to avoid being caught out by unexpected opening and closing hours, and to make sure you don't miss the celebrations!

It's worth spending time before you embark on your travels just looking through the topics to see what is covered and becoming familiar with what might be said to you.

Whatever the situation, your *Gem Phrasebook* is sure to help!

Contents

Pronouncing French

• •

In this book we have used a simple system to help you pronounce the phrases. We have designed the book so that as you read the pronunciation of the phrases you can follow the French. This will help you to recognize the different sounds and enable you to read French without relying on the guide. Here are a few rules you should know:

French	sounds like	example	pronunciation
au	oh	**autobus**	oh-toh-bews
c (+ a, o, u)	ka, ko, ku	**cas, col, cure**	ka, kol, kewr
c (+ e, i), ç	s	**ceci, ça**	suh-see, sa
ch	sh	**chat**	sha
é	ay	**été**	aytay
è	eh	**très**	treh
eau	oh	**beau**	boh
eu	uh	**neuf**	nuhf
g (+ e, i)	zhe, zhee	**gel, gîte**	zhel, zheet
gn	ny	**agneau**	a-nyoh
oi	wa	**roi**	rwa
u	ew	**sur**	sewr
ui	wee	**huit**	weet

e is sometimes weak and sounds like uh. This happens either in very short words (**je** zhuh, **le** luh, **se** suh, etc.) or when the **e** falls at the end of a syllable: **retard** ruh-tar, **depuis** duh-pwee.

h is not pronounced: **hôtel** oh-tel, **haricot** a-ree-koh.

There are nasal vowels in French (represented by **ñ**):
un uñ
fin/bain fañ/bañ
on oñ
dans/en dahñ/ahñ

Word endings are often silent: **Paris** pa-ree, **Londres** loñdr, **parlent** parl. However, the ending is sometimes pronounced if it is followed by a word which begins with a vowel:

avez-vous a-vay voo **but vous avez** voo za-vay.

In French, unlike English, there is normally no strong accent on any syllable, but instead a slight emphasis on the final syllable of each word, phrase and sentence, which takes the form of a rising intonation rather than an increase in volume.

Top ten tips

1 Use **vous** instead of **tu** until you are asked to use the familiar form. Do not use first names until you are invited.

2 Foreign visitors should not bring wine as a gift unless certain of its high quality.

3 Do not forget to stamp your train ticket before getting on the train – otherwise it will not be valid.

4 By law, French people must carry their ID cards all the time, and there might be ID inspections in the street (especially in big cities). The police will ask **'Vos papiers, s'il vous plaît'**.

5 Flowers should be given in odd numbers (but not 13). Do not send chrysanthemums (they are funeral flowers) or red roses (they have romantic connotations).

6 Keep your hands on the table at all times during a meal, do not place them on your lap. Elbows, however, should be kept off the table!

7   A glass of wine is filled to three-quarters, never to the brim.

8   When addressing a stranger, always add **Monsieur** or **Madame**, even if you are only asking for directions.

9   In some areas (especially the countryside) people do not speak a word of English, so have your phrasebook ready!

10 It is usually much appreciated when guests bring a bouquet for the lady of the house or chocolates for their hosts.

Talking to people

Hello/goodbye, yes/no

You will find the French quite formal in their greetings, shaking hands both on meeting and on parting. **Bonjour, madame** or **bonjour, monsieur** are the politest ways to greet someone. **Mademoiselle** is becoming less frequently used. **Salut** is more informal than **bonjour**. If someone offers you something, perhaps an extra serving of food, and you simply reply **merci**, they will take this to mean 'no'. You must say **oui, merci** or you will go hungry!

Please	**S'il vous plaît**
	seel voo pleh
Thanks	**Merci (beaucoup)**
(very much)	mehr-see (boh-koo)
You're welcome!	**De rien!**
	duh ryañ!
Yes	**Oui**
	wee
No	**Non**
	noñ

11

Yes, please	**Oui, merci**	
	wee, mehr-see	
No, thanks	**Non, merci**	
	noñ, mehr-see	
OK!	**D'accord!**	
	da-kor!	
Sir/Mr	**Monsieur/M.**	
	muh-syuh	
Madam/Mrs/Ms	**Madame/Mme**	
	ma-dam	
Miss	**Mademoiselle/Mlle**	
	mad-mwa-zel	
Hello/Hi	**Bonjour/Salut**	
	boñ-zhoor/sa-lew	
Goodbye/Bye	**Au revoir/Salut**	
	oh ruh-vwar/sa-lew	
Bye for now	**À bientôt**	
	a byañ-toh	
Good evening	**Bonsoir**	
	boñ-swar	
Goodnight	**Bonne nuit**	
	bon nwee	
See you tomorrow	**À demain**	
	a duh-mañ	
Excuse me! (to catch attention)	**Pardon, monsieur/madame!**	
	par-doñ, muh-syuh/ma-dam!	
Sorry!	**Pardon!**	
	par-doñ!	

I'm sorry	**Je suis désolé(e)**
	zhuh swee day-zo-lay
How are you?	**Comment allez-vous?**
	ko-mahñ ta-lay voo?
Fine, thanks	**Très bien, merci**
	treh byañ, mehr-see
And you?	**Et vous?**
	ay voo?
I don't understand	**Je ne comprends pas**
	zhuh nuh koñ-prahñ pa
I speak very little French	**Je parle très peu le français**
	zhuh parl treh puh luh frahñ-seh

Key phrases

. . . .

You don't need to say complicated things to get what you want. Often simply naming the thing and adding **s'il vous plaît** will do the trick, even when asking for directions.

the (masculine)	**le**
	luh
(feminine)	**la**
	la
(plural)	**les**
	lay

13

the museum	**le musée**
	luh mew-zay
the station	**la gare**
	la gar
the shops	**les magasins**
	lay ma-ga-zañ
a/one (masculine)	**un**
	uñ
(feminine)	**une**
	ewn
a ticket/	**un billet/un timbre**
one stamp	uñ bee-yeh/uñ tañbr
a room/	**une chambre/une bouteille**
one bottle	ewn shahñbr/ewn boo-tay-yuh
some (masculine)	**du**
	dew
(feminine)	**de la**
	duh la
(plural)	**des**
	day
some wine	**du vin**
	dew vañ
some jam	**de la confiture**
	duh la koñ-fee-tewr
some chips	**des frites**
	day freet
Do you have...?	**Est-ce que vous avez...?/**
	Vous avez...?
	es kuh voo za-vay...?/voo za-vay...?

Do you have a room?	**Est-ce que vous avez une chambre?**	
	es kuh voo za-vay ewn shahñbr?	
Do you have some milk?	**Vous avez du lait?**	
	voo za-vay dew leh?	
I'd like...	**Je voudrais...**	
	zhuh voo-dreh...	
We'd like...	**Nous voudrions...**	
	noo voo-dree-oñ...	
I'd like an ice cream	**Je voudrais une glace**	
	zhuh voo-dreh ewn glas	
We'd like to visit Paris	**Nous voudrions visiter Paris**	
	noo voo-dree-oñ vee-zee-tay pa-ree	
Some more...	**Encore du/de la/des...**	
	ahñ-kor dew/duh la/day...	
Another...	**Un/Une autre...**	
	uñ/ewn ohtr...	
Some more bread	**Encore du pain**	
	ahñ-kor dew pañ	
Some more soup	**Encore de la soupe**	
	ahñ-kor duh la soop	
Some more glasses	**Encore des verres**	
	ahñ-kor day vehr	
Another coffee	**Un autre café**	
	uñ nohtr ka-fay	
Another beer	**Une autre bière**	
	ewn ohtr byehr	
How much is it?	**C'est combien?**	
	say koñ-byañ?	

Key phrases

How much is the room?	**C'est combien la chambre?**
	say koñ-byañ la shahñbr?
large/small	**grand/petit**
	grahñ/puh-tee
with/without	**avec/sans**
	a-vek/sahñ
Where is/are...?	**Où est/sont...?**
	oo ay/soñ...?
the nearest	**le/la plus proche**
	luh/la plew prosh
How do I get...?	**Pour aller...?**
	poor a-lay...?
to the museum	**au musée**
	oh mew-zay
to the station	**à la gare**
	a la gar
to Brioude	**à Brioude**
	a bree-ood
There is/are...	**Il y a...**
	eel ya...
There isn't/ aren't any...	**Il n'y a pas de...**
	eel nya pa duh...
When...?	**Quand...?**
	kahñ...?
At what time...?	**À quelle heure...?**
	a kel ur...?
today	**aujourd'hui**
	oh-zhoor-dwee

tomorrow	**demain**	
	duh-mañ	
Can I...?	**Est-ce que je peux...?**	
	es kuh zhuh puh...?	
smoke	**fumer**	
	few-may	
What does this mean?	**Qu'est-ce que ça veut dire?**	
	kes kuh sa vuh deer?	

Signs and notices

entrée	entrance
sortie	exit
ouvert	open
fermé	closed
chaud	hot
froid	cold
tirez	pull
poussez	push
à droite	right
à gauche	left
eau potable	drinking water
à emporter	take-away
dégustation de vin	wine tasting
prière de...	please...
libre	free, vacant
occupé	engaged

caisse	cash desk
libre-service	self-service
toilettes	toilets
dames	ladies
hommes, messieurs	gents
hors service	out of order
à louer	for hire/to rent
à vendre	for sale
soldes	sale
baignade interdite	no bathing
sous-sol	basement
rez-de-chaussée	ground floor
ascenseur	lift
accès aux trains	to the trains
chambres	rooms available
complet	no vacancies
sortie de secours	emergency exit
sonnez	ring
appuyez	press
privé	private
arrêt	stop
billets	tickets
accueil	information
composter votre billet	validate your ticket
buffet	snacks
consigne	left luggage
non fumeurs	non-smoking
fumeurs	smoking
défense de fumer	no smoking

Polite expressions

• •

There are two forms of address in French, formal (**vous**) and informal (**tu**). You should always stick to the formal until you are invited to **tutoyer** (use the informal **tu**).

The meal was delicious	**Le repas était délicieux** luh ruh-pa ay-teh day-lee-syuh
Thank you very much	**Je vous remercie** zhuh voo ruh-mehr-see
Delighted to meet you	**Enchanté(e)** ahñ-shahñ-tay
This is...	**Voici...** vwa-see...
my husband/ my wife	**mon mari/ma femme** moñ ma-ree/ma fam
Enjoy your holiday!	**Passez de bonnes vacances!** pa-say duh bon va-kahñs!

Celebrations

•••••••••••••••••••••••••••••••

Christmas celebrations revolve more around food than presents. They start on Christmas Eve (**réveillon de Noël**) with a lavish meal (often seafood) lasting many hours. The main course for the actual Christmas lunch is usually goose or turkey followed by the traditional dessert, a **bûche de Noël** (Christmas log). Families start the celebrations with an **apéritif** before the meal accompanied by elaborate **amuse-bouche** (nibbles). Champagne sometimes replaces the usual **apéritif** drinks.

I'd like to wish you a...	**Je vous souhaite un/une...**
	zhuh voo soo-eht uñ/ewn...
Merry Christmas!	**Joyeux Noël!**
	zhwa-yuh noh-el!
Happy New Year!	**Bonne Année!**
	bon a-nay!
Happy Easter!	**Joyeuses Pâques!**
	zhwa-yuz pak!
Happy birthday!	**Bon anniversaire!**
	boñ na-nee-vehr-sehr!
Have a good trip!	**Bon voyage!**
	boñ vwa-yazh!
Enjoy your meal!	**Bon appétit!**
	boñ na-pay-tee!

Making friends

●●

In this section we have used the informal **tu** for the questions.

FACE TO FACE

A **Comment tu t'appelles?**
ko-mahñ tew ta-pel?
What's your name?

B **Je m'appelle...**
zhuh ma-pel...
My name is...

A **Tu es d'où?**
tew ay doo?
Where are you from?

B **Je suis anglais(e), de Londres**
zhuh swee zahñ-gleh(z), duh loñdr
I am English, from London

A **Enchanté(e)!**
ahñ-shahñ-tay!
Pleased to meet you!

How old are you?	**Quel âge as-tu?**	
	kel azh a tew?	
I'm ... years old	**J'ai ... ans**	
	zhay ... ahñ	
Are you French?	**Tu es français(e)?**	
	tew ay frahñ-seh(z)?	

21

I'm English/Scottish/American	**Je suis anglais(e)/écossais(e)/américain(e)** zhuh swee zahñ-gleh(z)/zay-ko-seh(z)/za-mayree-kañ/ken
Where do you live?	**Où est-ce que tu habites?** oo es kuh tew a-beet?
Where do you live? (plural)	**Où est-ce que vous habitez?** oo es kuh voo za-bee-tay?
I live in London	**J'habite à Londres** zha-beet a loñdr
We live in Glasgow	**Nous habitons à Glasgow** noo za-bee-toñ a glaz-goh
I'm...	**Je suis...** zhuh swee...
single	**célibataire** say-lee-ba-tehr
married	**marié(e)** mar-yay
divorced	**divorcé(e)** dee-vor-say
I have...	**J'ai...** zhay...
a boyfriend	**un petit ami** uñ puh-tee-ta-mee
a girlfriend	**une petite amie** ewn puh-teet a-mee

I have a partner (male/female)	**J'ai un compagnon/ une compagne**
	zhay uñ kom-pa-nyoñ/ ewn koñ-panyuh
I have ... children	**J'ai ... enfants**
	zhay ... ahñ-fahñ
I have no children	**Je n'ai pas d'enfants**
	zhuh nay pas dahñ-fahñ
I'm here on holiday/on business/for the weekend	**Je suis ici en vacances/ en voyage d'affaires/ en week-end**
	zhuh swee zee-see ahñ va-kahñs/ ahñ vwa-yazh da-fehr/ ahñ wee-kend

Work

●●●

What work do you do?	**Qu'est-ce que vous faites comme travail?**
	kes kuh voo fet kom tra-va-yuh?
I'm...	**Je suis...**
	zhuh swee...
a doctor	**médecin**
	may-dsañ

> **Leisure/interests** (p 71) > **Sport** (p 76)

a manager	**directeur**
	dee-rek-tur
a secretary	**secrétaire**
	suh-kray-tehr
I work from home	**Je travaille à domicile**
	zhuh tra-va-yuh a do-mee-seel
I'm self-employed	**Je travaille à mon compte**
	zhuh tra-va-yuh a moñ koñt

Weather

temps variable	changeable weather
tahñ va-ree-abl	
beau boh	fine
temps orageux	thundery weather
tahñ o-ra-zhuh	

It's sunny	**Il y a du soleil**
	eel ya dew so-lay
It's raining	**Il pleut**
	eel pluh
It's snowing	**Il neige**
	eel nezh
It's windy	**Il y a du vent**
	eel ya dew vahñ

What a lovely day!	**Quelle belle journée!**
	kel bel zhoor-nay!
What awful weather!	**Quel mauvais temps!**
	kel moh-veh tahñ!
What will the weather be like tomorrow?	**Quel temps fera-t-il demain?**
	kel tahñ fuh-ra-teel duh-mañ?
Do you think it's going to rain?	**Vous croyez qu'il va pleuvoir?**
	voo krwa-yay keel va pluh-vwar?
It's very hot/cold	**Il fait très chaud/froid**
	eel feh treh shoh/frwa

Getting around

Asking the way

en face de	ahñ fas duh	opposite
à côté de	a ko-tay duh	next to
près de	preh duh	near to
le carrefour	luh kar-foor	crossroad
le rond-point		roundabout
luh roñ-pwañ		

FACE TO FACE

A **Pardon, pour aller à la gare?**
par-doñ, poor a-lay a la gar?
Excuse me, how do I get to the station?

B **Continuez tout droit, après l'église tournez**
   à gauche/à droite
koñ-tee-new-ay too drwa, a-preh lay-gleez toor-nay
   a gohsh/a drwat
Keep straight on, after the church turn left/right

A C'est loin?
say lwañ?
Is it far?

B Non, c'est à deux cents mètres/à cinq minutes
noñ, say ta duh sahñ metr/a sañk mee-newt
No, 200 yards/five minutes

A Merci!
mehr-see!
Thank you!

B De rien!
duh ryañ!
You're welcome!

We're looking for...	**Nous cherchons...** noo shehr-shoñ...
Can we walk there?	**On peut y aller à pied?** oñ puh ee a-lay a pyay?
We're lost	**Nous nous sommes perdu(e)s** noo noo som pehr-dew
Is this the right way to...?	**C'est la bonne direction pour...?** say la bon dee-rek-syoñ poor...?
Can you show me on the map?	**Pouvez-vous me montrer sur la carte?** poo-vay voo me moñ-tray sewr la kart?

YOU MAY HEAR...	
C'est indiqué say tañ-dee-kay	It's signposted
C'est au coin de la rue say toh kwañ duh la rew	It's on the corner of the street
C'est là-bas say la-ba	It's over there

Bus and coach

∙∙

FACE TO FACE

A **Pardon, quel bus pour le centre-ville?**
par-doñ, kel bews poor luh sahñtr veel?
Excuse me, which bus goes to the centre?

B **Le 15**
luh kañz
Number 15

A **Où est l'arrêt?**
oo ay la-reh?
Where is the bus stop?

B **Là-bas, à gauche**
la-ba, a gohsh
There, on the left

A **Où est-ce que je peux acheter des tickets de bus?**
oo es kuh zhuh puh ash-tay day tee-keh duh bews?
Where can I buy bus tickets?

B **Là-bas, au distributeur**
la-ba, oh dees-tree-bew-tur
Over there, at the ticket machine

Is there a bus to...?	**Est-ce qu'il y a un bus pour...?** es keel ya uñ bews poor...?
Where do I catch the bus to go to...?	**Où est-ce qu'on prend le bus pour aller à/au (etc.)...?** oo es koñ prahñ luh bews poor a-lay a/oh...?
How much is it to...?	**C'est combien pour aller à/au (etc.)...?** say koñ-byañ poor a-lay a/oh...?
to the centre	**au centre** oh sahñtr
to the beach	**à la plage** a la plazh
to the shops	**aux magasins** oh ma-ga-zañ
to Montmartre	**à Montmartre** a moñ-martr
How frequent are the buses to...?	**Les bus pour ... passent tous les combien?** lay bews poor ... pas too lay koñ-byañ?

When is the first/ the last bus to...?	À quelle heure part le premier/le dernier bus pour...?
	a kel ur par luh pruh-myay/ luh dehr-nyay bews poor...?
Could you tell me when to get off?	Pourriez-vous me dire quand descendre?
	poo-ree-ay-voo muh deer kahñ deh-sahñdr?
This is my stop	C'est mon arrêt
	say moñ na-reh

YOU MAY HEAR...

Prenez le métro, c'est plus rapide	Take the metro, it's quicker
pruh-nay luh may-troh, say plew ra-peed	

> **Luggage** (p 92)

Metro

. . . .

In Paris ticket options include **un carnet de dix tickets** (a book of ten tickets), which can be used on metro, bus and RER (suburban metro), or **un billet de tourisme**, which covers seven days' travel.

entrée ahñ-tray	entrance
sortie sor-tee	way out/exit
la ligne de métro la lee-nyuh duh may-troh	metro line
en direction de... ahñ dee-rek-syoñ duh...	in the direction of...
correspondance ko-reh-spoñ-dahñs	connecting line

Where is the nearest metro?	**Où est la station de métro la plus proche?** oo ay la sta-syoñ duh may-troh la plew prosh?
I'm going to...	**Je vais à...** zhuh veh a...
How does the ticket machine work?	**Comment marche le guichet automatique?** ko-mahñ marsh luh gee-sheh oh-toh-ma-teek?

Do you have a map of the metro?	**Vous avez un plan du métro?** voo za-vay uñ plahñ dew may-troh?
How do I get to...?	**Pour aller à/au (etc.)...?** poor a-lay a/oh...?
Do I have to change?	**Est-ce qu'il faut changer?** es keel foh shañ-zhay?
Which line is it for...?	**C'est quelle ligne pour...?** say kel lee-nyuh poor...?
In which direction?	**Dans quelle direction?** dahñ kel dee-rek-syoñ?
What is the next stop?	**Quel est le prochain arrêt?** kel ay luh pro-shañ na-reh?

Train

Before you catch your train, you must validate your ticket in the machines situated on the platforms, which carry the warning **n'oubliez pas de composter votre billet**. Failing to do so could result in a fine that is more than the cost of the ticket. You can book tickets on the French Railways website **www.sncf.com**.

> **Luggage** (p 92)

horaire o-rehr	timetable
circuler seer-kew-lay	to operate
dimanches et fêtes dee-mahñsh ay fet	Sundays and holidays
accès aux quais ak-seh oh keh	to the platforms

FACE TO FACE

A **Quand part le prochain train pour…?**
kahñ par luh pro-shañ trañ poor…?
When is the next train to…?

B **A 17 heures 10**
a dee-set ur dees
At ten past five

A **Deux billets pour…**
duh bee-yeh poor…
Two tickets to…

B **Aller simple ou aller-retour?**
a-lay sañpl oo a-lay-ruh-toor?
Single or return?

First class/ Second class	**Première classe/ Deuxième classe** pruh myehr klas/duh-zyem klas
Smoking/ Non-smoking	**Fumeur/Non fumeur** few-mur/noñ few-mur

Is there a supplement to pay?	**Y a-t-il un supplément à payer?**
	ee a-teel uñ sew-play-mahñ a pay-yay?
I want to book a seat on the TGV to Nîmes	**Je voudrais réserver une place dans le TGV pour Nîmes**
	zhuh voo-dreh ray-zehr-vay ewn plas dahñ luh tay-zhay-vay poor neem
When is the train to...?	**Le train pour ... est à quelle heure?**
	luh trañ poor ... ay ta kel ur?
the first/the last	**le premier/le dernier**
	luh pruh myay/luh dehr-nyay
When does it arrive in...?	**À quelle heure arrive-t-il à...?**
	a kel ur a-reev-teel a....?
Do I have to change?	**Est-ce qu'il faut changer?**
	es keel foh shañ-zhay?
Which platform does it leave from?	**Il part de quel quai?**
	eel par duh kel kay?
Is this the right platform for the train to Paris?	**C'est le bon quai pour le train de Paris?**
	say luh boñ kay poor luh trañ duh pa-ree?
Is this the train for...?	**C'est le train pour...?**
	say luh trañ poor...?
When does it leave?	**Il part à quelle heure?**
	eel par a kel ur?

> **Luggage** (p 92)

Does the train stop at...?	**Est-ce que le train s'arrête à...?**
	es kuh luh trañ sa-ret a...?
Where do I change for...?	**Où dois-je changer pour...?**
	oo dwa-zhuh shahñ-zhay poor...?
Please tell me when we get to...	**S'il vous plaît, prévenez-moi quand nous serons à...**
	seel voo pleh, pray-vnay mwa kañ noo suh-roñ za...
Is this seat free?	**Cette place est-elle libre?**
	set plas ay-tel leebr?
Excuse me	**Excusez-moi**
	eks-kew-zay-mwa
Sorry!	**Pardon!**
	par-doñ!

Taxi

• •

| **la station de taxis** | taxi rank |
| la sta-syoñ duh tak-see | |

I want a taxi	**Je voudrais un taxi**
	zhuh voo-dreh uñ tak-see
Where can I get a taxi?	**Où est-ce que je peux prendre un taxi?**
	oo es kuh zhuh puh prahñdr uñ tak-see?

Could you order me a taxi?	**Pouvez-vous m'appeler un taxi?**
	poo-vay voo ma-play uñ tak-see?
How much is it going to cost to go to...?	**Combien ça va coûter pour aller à/au (etc.)...?**
	koñ-byañ sa va koo-tay poor a-lay a/oh...?
to the town centre	**au centre-ville**
	oh sahñtr-veel
to the station	**à la gare**
	a la gar
to the airport	**à l'aéroport**
	a la-ay-ro-por
to this address	**à cette adresse**
	a set a-dres
How much is it?	**C'est combien?**
	say koñ-byañ?
It's more than on the meter	**C'est plus qu'au compteur**
	say plew skoh koñ-tur
Keep the change	**Gardez la monnaie**
	gar-day la mo-neh
Sorry, I don't have any change	**Je suis désolé(e), je n'ai pas de monnaie**
	zhuh swee day-zo-lay, zhuh nay pa duh mo-neh
I'm in a hurry	**Je suis pressé(e)**
	zhuh swee preh-say
Is it far?	**C'est loin?**
	say lwañ?

> **Luggage** (p 92)

Boat and ferry

....

When is the next boat/ferry to...?	**À quelle heure part le prochain bateau/ferry pour...?** a kel ur par luh pro-shañ ba-toh/ feh-ree poor...?
Have you a timetable?	**Vous avez un horaire?** voo za-vay uñ noh-rehr?
Is there a car ferry to...?	**Est-ce qu'il y a un car ferry pour...?** es keel ya uñ car feh-ree poor...?
How much is...?	**C'est combien...?** seh koñ-byañ...?
a single	**un aller simple** uñ na-lay sañpl
a return	**un aller-retour** uñ na-lay-ruh-toor
A tourist ticket	**Un billet touristique** uñ bee-yeh too-rees-teek
How much is it for a car and ... people?	**C'est combien pour une voiture et ... personnes?** say koñ-byañ poor ewn vwa-tewr ay ... pehr-son?
How long is the crossing?	**La traversée dure combien de temps?** la tra-vehr-say dewr koñ-byañ duh tahñ?
Where does the boat leave from?	**D'où part le bateau?** doo par luh ba-toh?

When is the first/ last boat?	**Le premier/dernier bateau part quand?**
	luh pruh-myay/dehr-nyay ba-toh par kahñ?
What time do we get to...?	**On arrive à quelle heure à...?**
	on a-reev a kel ur a...?
Is there somewhere to eat on the boat?	**Est-ce qu'on peut manger sur le bateau?**
	es koñ puh mahñ-zhay sewr luh ba-toh?

Air travel

How do I get to the airport?	**Comment fait-on pour aller à l'aéroport?**
	ko-mahñ fay toñ poor a-lay a la-ay-ro-por?
How long does it take to get to the airport?	**On met combien de temps pour aller à l'aéroport?**
	oñ meh koñ-byañ duh tahñ poor a-lay a la-ay-ro-por?
How much is the taxi fare...?	**C'est combien le taxi pour aller...?**
	say koñ-byañ luh tak-see poor a-lay...?
into town	**en ville**
	ahñ veel
to the hotel	**à l'hôtel**
	a loh-tel

Is there an airport bus to the city centre?	**Est-ce qu'il y a une navette pour aller au centre-ville?**
	es keel ya ewn na-vet poor a-lay oh sahñtr-veel?
Where do I check in for...?	**Où est l'enregistrement pour...?**
	oo ay lahñ-ruh-zhee-struh-mahñ poor...?
Where is the luggage for the flight from...?	**Où sont les bagages du vol en provenance de...?**
	oo soñ lay ba-gazh dew vol ahñ pro-vnahñs duh...?
Which is the departure gate for the flight to...?	**Quelle est la porte d'embarquement pour le vol à destination de...?**
	kel ay la port dahñ-bar-kuh-mahñ poor luh vol a des-tee-na-syoñ duh...?

YOU MAY HEAR...

L'embarquement aura lieu porte numéro... lahñ-bar-kuh-mahñ oh-ra lyuh port new-may-ro...	Boarding will take place at gate number...
Présentez-vous immédiatement porte numéro... pray-zahñ-tay voo ee-may-dyat-mahñ port new-may-ro...	Go immediately to gate number...
Votre vol a du retard votr vol a dew ruh-tar	Your flight is delayed

> **Luggage** (p 92)

39

Customs control

• •

With the Single European Market, European Union (EU)
citizens are subject only to spot checks and can go
through the blue customs channel (unless they have
goods to declare). There is no restriction, in either
quantity or value, on goods purchased by EU travellers
in another EU country provided that they are for
personal use.

Getting around

contrôle des passeports koñ-trol day pas-por	passport control
UE (Union Européenne) ew uh	EU (European Union)
autres passeports ohtr pas-por	other passports
douane dwan	customs

Do I have to pay duty on this?	**Est-ce que je dois payer des droits de douane sur ça?** es kuh zhuh dwa pay-yay day drwa duh dwan sewr sa?
It is for my own personal use	**C'est pour mon usage personnel** say poor moñ new-zazh pehr-so-nel
We are on our way to... (if in transit through a country)	**Nous allons en/au/aux...** noo za-loñ ahñ/oh/oh...

Driving

Car hire

le permis de conduire luh pehr-mee duh koñ-dweer	driving licence
l'assurance la-sew-rahñs	insurance

I want to hire a car	**Je voudrais louer une voiture** zhuh voo-dreh loo-ay ewn vwa-tewr
for ... days	**pour ... jours** poor ... zhoor
for the weekend	**pour le week-end** poor luh wee-kend
What are your rates...?	**Quels sont vos tarifs...?** kel soñ voh ta-reef...?
per day	**par jour** par zhoor
per week	**par semaine** par suh-men

Is there a mileage (kilometre) charge?	**Est-ce que le kilométrage est en plus?** es kuh luh kee-lo-may-trazh ay tahñ plews?
How much is it?	**C'est combien?** say koñ-byañ?
Does the price include comprehensive insurance?	**Est-ce que le prix comprend l'assurance tous-risques?** es kuh luh pree koñ-prahñ la-sew-rahñs too reesk?
Must I return the car here?	**Est-ce que je dois rendre la voiture ici?** es kuh zhuh dwa rahñdr la vwa-tewr ee-see?
By what time?	**Vers quelle heure?** vehr kel ur?
I'd like to leave it in...	**Je voudrais la laisser à...** zhuh voo-dreh la leh-say a...
What do I do if we break down?	**Que dois-je faire en cas de panne?** kuh dwa-zhuh fehr ahñ ka duh pan?

YOU MAY HEAR...

Veuillez rendre la voiture avec un plein d'essence vuh-yay rahñdr la vwa-tewr a-vek uñ plañ deh-sahñs	Please return the car with a full tank

Driving

•••••••••••••••••••••••••••••••••••••

I am looking for a car park	**Je cherche un parking** zhuh shehrsh uñ par-keeng
Do I need to pay?	**Il faut payer?** eel foh pay-ay?
Can I park here?	**On peut se garer ici?** oñ puh suh ga-ray ee-see?
How long can I park for?	**Combien de temps peut-on se garer ici?** koñ-byañ duh tahñ puh-toñ suh ga-ray ee-see?
Is the road good?	**Est-ce que la route est bonne?** es kuh la root ay bon?
Can you show me on the map?	**Pouvez-vous me montrer sur la carte?** poo-vay voo muh moñ-tray sewr la kart?

Petrol

•••

sans plomb sahñ ploñ	unleaded
diesel/gasoil dee-eh-zel/ga-zwal	diesel

Fill it up, please	**Le plein, s'il vous plaît** luh plañ, seel voo pleh
Please check the oil/the water	**Pouvez-vous vérifier l'huile/l'eau?** poo-vay voo vay-ree-fyay lweel/loh?
...euros' worth of unleaded petrol	**...euros d'essence sans plomb** ...uh-roh deh-sahñs sahñ ploñ
Pump number...	**La pompe numéro...** la pomp new-may-roh...
Can you check the tyre pressure?	**Pouvez-vous vérifier la pression des pneus?** Poo-vay voo vay-ree-fyay la preh-syoñ day pnuh?
Where do I pay?	**Où dois-je payer?** oo dwa-zhuh pay-yay?
Do you take credit cards?	**Vous acceptez les cartes de crédit?** voo zak-sep-tay lay kart duh kray-dee?

44

Breakdown

● ●

assistance automobile a-sees-tahñs oh-toh-mo-beel	breakdown assistance

Can you help me? **Pouvez-vous m'aider?**
poo-vay voo may-day?

My car has broken **Ma voiture est en panne**
down ma vwa-tewr ay tahñ pan

I can't start the **Je n'arrive pas à démarrer**
car zhuh na-reev pa a day-ma-ray

I've run out of **Je suis en panne d'essence**
petrol zhuh swee ahñ pan deh-sahñs

Is there a garage **Il y a un garage près d'ici?**
near here? eel ya uñ ga-razh preh dee-see?

Can you tow me **Pouvez-vous me remorquer**
to the nearest **jusqu'au garage le plus**
garage? **proche?**
Poo-vay voo muh ruh-mor-kay
zhew-skoh ga-razh luh plew prosh?

Do you have **Avez-vous des pièces de**
parts for a **rechange pour une...?**
(make of car) a-vay voo day pyes duh
ruh-shahñzh poor ewn...?

There's **J'ai un problème avec**
something **le/la/les...**
wrong with zhay uñ prob-lem a-vek
the... luh/la/lay...

Car parts

....

The ... doesn't work | **Le/La/L' ... ne marche pas**
luh/la/l ... nuh marsh pa
The ... don't work | **Les ... ne marchent pas**
lay ... nuh marsh pa

accelerator	l'accélérateur	ak-say-lay-ra-tur
battery	la batterie	ba-tree
bonnet	le capot	ka-poh
brakes	les freins	frañ
choke	le starter	star-tehr
clutch	l'embrayage	ahñ-bray-yazh
distributor	le delco	del-koh
engine	le moteur	mo-tur
exhaust pipe	le pot d'échappement	poh day-shap-mahñ
fuse	le fusible	few-zeebl
gears	les vitesses	vee-tes
handbrake	le frein à main	frañ a mañ
headlights	les phares	far
ignition	l'allumage	a-lew-mazh
indicator	le clignotant	klee-nyo-tahñ
points	les vis platinées	vees pla-tee-nay
radiator	le radiateur	ra-dya-tur
reversing lights	les phares de recul	far duh ruh-kewl

Driving

46

seat belt	**la ceinture de sécurité**	sañ-tewr duh say-kewr-eetay
sidelights	**les veilleuses**	vay-yuhz
spare wheel	**la roue de secours**	roo duh skoor
spark plugs	**les bougies**	boo-zhee
steering	**la direction**	dee-rek-syoñ
steering wheel	**le volant**	vo-lahñ
tyre	**le pneu**	pnuh
wheel	**la roue**	roo
windscreen	**le pare-brise**	par-breez
windscreen washers	**le lave-glace**	lav-glas
windscreen wiper	**l'essuie-glace**	es-wee-glas

Road signs

DOUANE / ZOLL
customs

HALTE / PEAGE
toll station for motorway

CÉDEZ LE PASSAGE
give way

RALENTIR
slow down

SENS UNIQUE
one way

Déviation
diversion

priority road

north
Nord

west **Ouest**

east **Est**

Sud
south

libre
spaces

complet
full

no parking

switch on
your lights

speeds are in
kilometers per hour

motorway

Staying somewhere

Hotel (booking)

You can book accommodation over the internet using the French Tourist Office website, **www.franceguide.com**.

a single room	**une chambre pour une personne**
	ewn shañbr poor ewn pehr-son
a double room	**une chambre pour deux personnes**
	ewn shañbr poor duh pehr-son
with bath	**avec bain**
	a-vek bañ
with shower	**avec douche**
	a-vek doosh
with a double bed	**à un lit**
	a uñ lee
twin-bedded	**à deux lits**
	a duh lee
with an extra bed for a child	**avec un autre lit pour un enfant**
	avek uñ nohtr lee poor uñ nahñ-fahñ

A **Je voudrais (réserver) une chambre pour une/deux personnes**
zhuh voo-dreh (ray-zehr-vay) ewn shahñbr poor ewn/duh pehr-son
I'd like (to book) a single/double room

B **C'est pour combien de nuits?**
say poor koñ-byañ duh nwee?
For how many nights?

A **Pour une nuit/... nuits**
poor ewn nwee/... nwee
For one night/... nights

B **Du... au...**
dew... oh...
From... till...

A **C'est pour combien de personnes?**
say poor koñ-byañ duh pehr-son?
For how many people?

B **Pour une personne/... personnes**
poor ewn pehr-son/... pehr-son
For one person/... people

Do you have a room for tonight?	**Est-ce que vous avez une chambre pour ce soir?** es kuh voo za-vay ewn shahñbr poor suh swar?
How much is it per night/ per week?	**C'est combien par nuit/ par semaine?** say koñ-byañ par nwee/par suh-men?

I'll arrive at...	**J'arriverai à...**
	zha-ree-vuh-ray a...
Do you have a list of hotels with prices?	**Vous avez une liste des hôtels avec leurs prix?**
	Voo za-vay ewn leest day zoh-tel a-vek lur pree?
Could you recommend a good hotel?	**Pouvez-vous me conseiller un bon hôtel?**
	poo-vay voo muh koñ-say-yay uñ boñ noh-tel?
not too expensive	**pas trop cher**
	pa troh shehr

YOU MAY HEAR...	
C'est complet	We're full
say koñ-pleh	
Votre nom, s'il vous plaît?	Your name, please?
votr noñ, seel voo pleh?	
Veuillez confirmer...	Please confirm...
vuh-yay koñ-feer-may...	
par e-mail	by e-mail
par ee-mehl	
par fax	by fax
par fax	
Vous arriverez à quelle heure?	What time will you arrive?
voo za-reev-ray a kel ur?	

52

Hotel desk

You generally have to fill in a registration form (**fiche d'étranger**) and give your passport number on arrival.

I booked a room	**J'ai réservé une chambre**
	zhay ray-zehr-vay ewn shahñbr
My name is...	**Je m'appelle...**
	zhuh ma-pel...
Have you anything else?	**Vous avez autre chose?**
	voo za-vay ohtr shoz?
Where can I park the car?	**Où est-ce que je peux garer la voiture?**
	oo es kuh zhuh puh ga-ray la vwa-tewr?
What time is...?	**À quelle heure est...?**
	a kel ur eh...?
dinner	**le dîner**
	luh dee-nay
breakfast	**le petit-déjeuner**
	luh puh-tee day-zhuh-nay
The key, please	**La clé/clef, s'il vous plaît**
	la klay, seel voo pleh
Room number...	**Chambre numéro...**
	shahñbr new-may-ro...
I'm leaving tomorrow	**Je pars demain**
	zhuh par duh-mañ
Please prepare the bill	**Pouvez-vous préparer la note?**
	poo-vay voo pray-pa-ray la not?

Camping

ordures or-dewr	rubbish
eau potable oh po-tabl	drinking water
bloc sanitaire blok sa-nee-tehr	washing facilities

Is there a restaurant on the campsite?	**Y a-t-il un restaurant dans le camping?** ee a-teel uñ re-sto-rahñ dahñ luh kahñ-peeng?
Do you have any vacancies?	**Vous avez des emplacements de libre?** Voo za-vay day zahñ-plas-mahñ duh leebr?
Does the price include...?	**Est-ce que le prix comprend...?** es kuh luh pree koñ-prahñ...?
hot water	**l'eau chaude** loh shohd
electricity	**l'électricité** lay-lek-tree-see-tay
We'd like to stay for ... nights	**Nous voudrions rester ... nuits** noo voo-dree-yoñ res-tay ... nwee
How much is it per night...?	**C'est combien la nuit...?** say koñ-byañ la nwee...?
for a tent	**pour une tente** poor ewn tahñt
for a caravan	**pour une caravane** poor ewn ka-ra-van

54

Self-catering

....

You can find a variety of self-catering accommodation on **www.gites-de-france.fr**, the website of the national Gîtes de France federation.

Who do we contact if there are problems?
Qui devons-nous contacter en cas de problème?
kee duh-voñ noo koñ-tak-tay ahñ ka duh prob-lehm?

How does the heating work?
Comment marche le chauffage?
ko-mahñ marsh luh shoh-fazh?

Is there always hot water?
Est-ce qu'il y a de l'eau chaude en permanence?
es keel ya duh loh shohd ahñ pe-rma-nahñs?

Where is the nearest supermarket?
Où est le supermarché le plus proche?
oo ay luh sew-pehr-mar-shay luh plew prosh?

Where do we leave the rubbish?
Où est-ce qu'il faut mettre les ordures?
oo es keel foh metr lay zor-dewr?

> **Sightseeing and tourist office** (p 69)

Shopping

Shopping phrases

French shop opening hours are approximately 9 am to 7 pm, but many shops close for lunch (between 12 and 2 pm) and most are closed on Sundays and Mondays.

FACE TO FACE

A **Qu'est-ce que vous désirez?**
kes kuh voo day-zee-ray?
What would you like?

B **Est-ce que vous avez...?**
es kuh voo za-vay...?
Do you have...?

A **Oui, bien sûr. Voilà. Et avec ceci?**
wee, byañ sewr. vwa-la. ay a-vek suh-see?
Yes, certainly. Here you are. Anything else?

56

Where is...?	**Où est...?**
	oo ay...?
I'm looking for a present for...	**Je cherche un cadeau pour...**
	zhuh shehrsh uñ ka-doh poor...
my mother	**ma mère**
	ma mehr
a child	**un enfant**
	uñ nahñ-fahñ
Where can I buy...?	**Où est-ce qu'on peut acheter...?**
	oo es koñ puh ash-tay...?
toys	**des jouets**
	day zhoo-ay
gifts	**des cadeaux**
	day ka-doh
Where is the ... department?	**Où se trouve le rayon...?**
	oo suh troov luh ray-yoñ...?
perfume	**parfumerie**
	par-few-mree
jewellery	**bijouterie**
	bee-zhoo-tree
I'd like something similar to this	**Je voudrais quelque chose dans ce genre-là**
	zhuh voo-dreh kel-kuh shohz dahñ suh zhahñr la
It's too expensive for me	**C'est trop cher pour moi**
	say troh shehr poor mwa
Have you anything else?	**Vous n'avez rien d'autre?**
	voo na-vay ryañ dohtr?

Shops

magasin ma-ga-zañ	shop
soldes sold	sale
un acheté, un gratuit uñ nash-tay, uñ gra-twee	buy one, get one free
le rayon alimentation luh ray-oñ a-lee-mahñ-ta-syoñ	the food department

baker's	**la boulangerie**	boo-lahñzh-ree
bookshop	**la librairie**	lee-breh-ree
butcher's	**la boucherie**	boo-shree
cake shop	**la pâtisserie**	pa-tee-sree
cheese shop	**la fromagerie**	fro-mazh-ree
clothes shop	**le magasin de vêtements**	ma-ga-zañ duh vetmahñ
dry-cleaner's	**le pressing**	pres-eeng
gift shop	**le magasin de cadeaux**	ma-ga-zañ duh ka-doh
greengrocer's	**le magasin de fruits et légumes**	ma-ga-zañ duh frwee zay lay-gewm
grocer's	**l'épicerie**	ay-pees-ree
hairdresser's	**chez le coiffeur/ la coiffeuse**	shay luh kwa-fur/ la kwa-fuz
hypermarket	**l'hypermarché**	ee-pehr-mar-shay

jeweller's	**la bijouterie**	bee-zhoot-ree
market	**le marché**	mar-shay
pharmacy/ chemist's	**la pharmacie**	far-ma-see
self-service	**le libre-service**	leebr-sehr-vees
shoe shop	**le magasin de chaussures**	ma-ga-zañ duh shoh-sewr
supermarket	**le supermarché**	sew-pehr-mar-shay
tobacconist's	**le tabac**	ta-ba

Food (general)

bread	**le pain**	pañ
bread stick (large)	**le pain**	pañ
bread stick (small)	**la baguette**	ba-get
bread roll	**le petit pain**	puh-tee pañ
butter	**le beurre**	bur
cheese	**le fromage**	fro-mazh
chicken	**le poulet**	poo-leh
coffee (instant)	**le café (instantané)**	ka-fay (añ-stahñ-ta-nay)
cream	**la crème**	krem
crisps	**les chips**	sheeps
eggs	**les œufs**	uh

fish	**le poisson**	pwa-soñ
flour	**la farine**	fa-reen
ham (cooked)	**le jambon cuit**	zhahñ-boñ kwee
ham (cured)	**le jambon cru**	zhahñ-boñ kru
honey	**le miel**	myel
jam	**la confiture**	koñ-fee-tewr
margarine	**la margarine**	mar-ga-reen
marmalade	**la confiture d'orange**	koñ-fee-tewr do-rahñzh
milk	**le lait**	leh
oil	**l'huile**	weel
orange juice	**le jus d'orange**	zhew do-rahñzh
pasta	**les pâtes**	pat
pepper	**le poivre**	pwavr
rice	**le riz**	ree
salt	**le sel**	sel
sugar	**le sucre**	sewkr
tea	**le thé**	tay
yoghurt	**le yaourt**	ya-oort

> **Measurements and quantities** (p 113)

Food (fruit and veg)

Fruit

fruit	**les fruits**	frwee
apples	**les pommes**	pom
bananas	**les bananes**	ba-nan
cherries	**les cerises**	suh-reez
grapefruit	**le pamplemousse**	pahñ-pluh-moos
grapes	**le raisin**	reh-zañ
lemon	**le citron**	see-troñ
melon	**le melon**	muh-loñ
nectarines	**les nectarines**	nek-ta-reen
oranges	**les oranges**	o-rahñzh
peaches	**les pêches**	pesh
pears	**les poires**	pwahr
pineapple	**l'ananas**	a-na-nas
plums	**les prunes**	prewn
raspberries	**les framboises**	frahñ-bwaz
strawberries	**les fraises**	frez

Vegetables

vegetables	**les légumes**	lay-gewm
carrots	**les carottes**	ka-rot
cauliflower	**le chou-fleur**	shoo-flur
courgettes	**les courgettes**	koor-zhet
French beans	**les haricots verts**	a-ree-koh vehr

61

garlic	l'ail	a-yuh
lettuce	la laitue	leh-tew
mushrooms	les champignons	shahñ-pee-nyoñ
onions	les oignons	o-nyoñ
peas	les petits pois	puh-tee pwa
peppers	les poivrons	pwa-vroñ
potatoes	les pommes de terre	pom duh tehr
spinach	les épinards	ay-pee-nar
tomatoes	les tomates	to-mat

Clothes

• •

Size for clothes is **la taille** (ta-yuh); for shoes it is
la pointure (pwañ-tewr).

FACE TO FACE

A **Est-ce que je peux l'essayer?**
es kuh zhuh puh leh-say-yay?
May I try this on?

B **Certainement, par ici, s'il vous plaît**
sehr-ten-mahñ, par ee-see seel voo pleh
Certainly, please come this way

> **Paying** (p 90) > **Numbers** (p 115)

A **L'avez-vous en plus grand/en plus petit?**
la-vay voo ahñ plew grahñ/ahñ plew puh-tee?
Do you have it in a bigger size/in a smaller size?

B **Désolé(e), je n'ai que cette taille dans ce coloris**
day-zo-lay, zhuh nay kuh set ta-yuh dahñ suh ko-lo-ree
Sorry, we only have this size in this colour

Do you have this in any other colours?	**Est-ce que vous l'avez dans d'autres coloris?** es kuh voo la-vay dahñ dohtr ko-lo-ree?
That's a shame!	**C'est dommage!** say do-mazh!
It's too...	**C'est trop...** say troh...
short	**court** koor
long	**long** loñ
I'm just looking	**Je regarde seulement** zhuh ruh-gard suhl-mahñ
I'll take it	**Je le prends** zhuh luh prahñ

| Quelle pointure faites-vous?
kel pwañ-tewr feht voo? | What shoe size do you take? |
| Quelle est votre taille?
kel eh votr ta-yuh? | What size (clothes) are you? |

Clothes (articles)

● ●

le coton luh ko-toñ	cotton
la soie la swa	silk
la dentelle la dahñ-tel	lace
la laine la lehn	wool

blouse	le chemisier	shuh-mee-zyay
bra	le soutien-gorge	soo-tyañ gorzh
coat	le manteau	mahñ-toh
dress	la robe	rob
gloves	les gants	gahñ
hat	le chapeau	sha-poh
jacket	la veste	vest
knickers	le slip	sleep
nightdress	la chemise de nuit	shuh-meez duh nwee
pyjamas	le pyjama	pee-zha-ma

Shopping

raincoat	l'imperméable	añ-pehr-may-abl
sandals	les sandales	sahñ-dal
scarf (silk)	le foulard	foo-lar
scarf (woollen)	l'écharpe	ay-sharp
shirt	la chemise	shuh-meez
shoes	les chaussures	shoh-sewr
shorts	le short	short
skirt	la jupe	zhewp
socks	les chaussettes	shoh-set
suit (woman's)	le tailleur	ta-yur
suit (man's)	le costume	kos-tewm
swimsuit	le maillot de bain	ma-yoh duh bañ
tights	les collants	ko-lahñ
t-shirt	le t-shirt	tee-shurt
tracksuit	le survêtement	sewr-vet-mahñ
trainers	les baskets	bas-ket
trousers	le pantalon	pahñ-ta-loñ

Maps and guides

. . . .

Do you have...?	**Avez-vous...?**
	a-vay vooz...?
a map of the town	**un plan de la ville**
	uñ plahñ duh la veel
a map of the region	**une carte de la région**
	ewn kart duh la ray-zhyoñ

> **Paying** (p 90)   65

Can you show me where ... is on the map?	**Pouvez-vous me montrer où est ... sur la carte?**
	poo-vay voo muh moñ-tray oo eh ... sewr la kart?
Do you have a detailed map of the area?	**Vous avez une carte détaillée de la région?**
	voo za-vay ewn kart day-ta-yay duh la ray-zhyoñ?
Do you have a guide book/leaflet in English?	**Vous avez un guide/une brochure en anglais?**
	voo za-vay uñ geed/ewn bro-shewr ahñ nahñ-gleh?
Where can I/we buy an English newspaper?	**Où est-ce qu'on peut acheter des journaux anglais?**
	oo es koñ puh ash-tay day zhoor-noh ahñ-gleh?
Do you have any English newspapers/any English novels?	**Vous avez des journaux anglais/des romans anglais?**
	voo za-vay day zhoor-noh ahñ-gleh/day ro-mahñ ahñ-gleh?

Post office

● ●

Smaller post offices generally shut for lunch (12 to 2 pm).

| **la poste** | la post | post office |
| **timbres** | tañbr | stamps |

66

> **Sightseeing** (p 69)

Is there a post office near here?	**Il y a un bureau de poste près d'ici?**
	eel ya uñ bewr-oh duh post preh dee-see?
When is it open?	**Il ouvre quand?**
	eel oovr kahñ?
Which counter is it...?	**C'est quel guichet...?**
	say kel gee-shay...?
for stamps	**pour les timbres**
	poor lay tañbr
for parcels	**pour les colis**
	poor lay ko-lee
Three stamps for postcards to Great Britain	**Trois timbres pour cartes postales pour la Grande-Bretagne**
	trwa tañbr poor kart pos-tal poor la grahñd bruh-ta-nyuh
How much is it to send this parcel?	**C'est combien pour envoyer ce colis?**
	say koñ-byañ poor ahñ-vwa-yay suh ko-lee?

YOU MAY HEAR...

| **Vous pouvez acheter des timbres au tabac** | You can buy stamps at the tobacconist's |
| voo poo-vay ash-tay day tañbr oh ta-ba | |

> **Money** (p 89) > **Paying** (p 90)

Photos

••••••••••••••••••••••••••••••••••••

Tapes and memory cards for cameras, video cameras and camcorders can be bought in supermarkets and photo and hi-fi shops (**magasin hi-fi**).

A video tape for this camcorder, please
Une cassette vidéo pour ce caméscope, s'il vous plaît
ewn ka-set vee-day-oh poor suh ka-may-skop, seel voo pleh

Do you have batteries for...?
Avez-vous des piles pour...?
a-vay voo day peel poor...?

this camera/ this camcorder
cet appareil/ce caméscope
set a-pa-ray/suh ka-may-skop

Do you have a memory card for...?
Avez-vous une carte mémoire pour...?
a-vay voo ewn kart may-mwar poor...?

this digital camera
cet appareil numérique
set a-pa-ray new-may-reek

Leisure

Sightseeing and tourist office

• •

The tourist office is sometimes called **le syndicat d'initiative**, but usually **l'office de/du tourisme**. If you are looking for somewhere to stay, a tourist office will have details of hotels, campsites, etc. Most museums are closed on Tuesdays.

Where is the tourist office?	**Où est l'office de tourisme?**
	oo eh lo-fees duh too-reesm?
What is there to visit in the area?	**Qu'est-ce qu'il y a à voir dans la région?**
	kes keel ya a war dahñ la ray-zhyoñ?
in ... hours	**en ... heures**
	ahñ ... ur
Do you have any leaflets?	**Avez-vous de la documentation?**
	a-vay voo duh la do-kew-mahñ-ta-syoñ?

69

Are there any excursions?	**Est-ce qu'il y a des excursions?**
	es keel ya day zek-skewr-syoñ?
We'd like to go to...	**On voudrait aller à...**
	oñ voo-dreh a-lay a...
How much does it cost to get in?	**C'est combien l'entrée?**
	say koñ-byañ lahñ-tray?
Are there any reductions for...?	**Est-ce que vous faites des réductions pour...?**
	es kuh voo feht day ray-dewk-syoñ poor...?
children	**les enfants**
	lay zahñ-fahñ
students	**les étudiants**
	lay zay-tew-dyahñ
the unemployed	**les chômeurs**
	lay shoh-mur
senior citizens	**les retraités**
	lay ruh-treh-tay

> **Maps and guides** (p 65)

Entertainment

. . . .

Check at the local tourist office for information
about local events. You can also find listings on
www.franceguide.com.

What is there to do in the evenings?	**Qu'est-ce qu'on peut faire le soir?**
	kes koñ puh fehr luh swar?
Do you have a list of events for this month?	**Vous avez une liste des festivités pour ce mois-ci?**
	Voo za-vay ewn leest day fes-tee-vee-tay poor suh mwa-see?
Is there anything for children to do?	**Est-ce qu'il y a des choses à faire pour les enfants?**
	es keel ya day shohz a fehr poor lay zahñ-fahñ?

Leisure/interests

. . . .

Where can I/we...?	**Où est-ce qu'on peut...?**
	oo es koñ puh...?
go fishing	**pêcher**
	peh-shay

go riding	**faire du cheval**
	fehr dew shuh-val
Are there any good (sandy) beaches near here?	**Est-ce qu'il y a de bonnes plages (de sable) près d'ici?**
	es keel ya duh bon plazh duh sabl preh dee-see?
Is there a swimming pool?	**Est-ce qu'il y a une piscine?**
	es keel ya ewn pee-seen?

Music

....

Are there any good concerts on?	**Il y a de bons concerts en ce moment?**
	eel ya duh boñ koñ-sehr ahñ suh mo-mahñ?
Where can I get tickets for the concert?	**Où est-ce qu'on peut avoir des billets pour le concert?**
	oo es koñ puh av-war day bee-yeh poor luh koñ-sehr?
Where can we hear some classical music/ some jazz?	**Où est-ce qu'on peut aller écouter de la musique classique/du jazz?**
	oo es koñ puh a-lay ay-koo-tay duh la mew-zeek kla-seek/dew jaz?

> **Making friends** (p 21)

Cinema

sous-titré soo-tee-tray	subtitled	
la séance la sayahñs	performance	
VO (version originale) vehr-syoñ o-ree-zhee-nal	in the original language (i.e. not dubbed)	

What's on at the cinema?	**Qu'est-ce qui passe au cinéma?** kes kee pas oh see-nay-ma?
When does the film start/finish?	**Le film commence/finit à quelle heure?** luh feelm ko-mahñs/fee-nee a kel ur?
How much are the tickets?	**C'est combien les billets?** say koñ-byañ lay bee-yeh?
I'd like two seats at ... euros	**Je voudrais deux places à ... euros** zhuh voo-dreh duh plas a ... uh-roh

Theatre/opera

la pièce la pyes	play	
la représentation la ruh-pray-zahñ-ta-syoñ	performance	

à l'orchestre	a lor-kestr	in the stalls
au balcon	oh bal-koñ	in the circle
le fauteuil		seat
luh foh-tuh-yuh		
le vestiaire	luh ves-tyehr	cloakroom
l'entracte	lahñ-trakt	interval

What is on at the theatre/at the opera?
Qu'est-ce qu'on joue au théâtre/à l'opéra?
kes koñ zhoo oh tay-atr/
a lo-pay-ra?

What prices are the tickets?
Les billets sont à combien?
lay bee-yeh soñ ta koñ-byañ?

I'd like two tickets...
Je voudrais deux billets...
zhuh voo-dreh duh bee-yeh...

for tonight
pour ce soir
poor suh swar

for tomorrow night
pour demain soir
poor duh-mañ swar

for 5th August
pour le cinq août
poor luh sañk oo(t)

When does the performance begin/end?
Quand est-ce que la représentation commence/finit?
kahñ tes kuh la
ruh-pray-zahñ-ta-syoñ
ko-mahñs/fee-nee?

Television

....

la télécommande tay-lay-ko-mahñd	remote control
le feuilleton luh fuh-yuh-toñ	soap
les informations lay zañ-for-ma-syoñ	news
mettre en marche metr ahñ marsh	to switch on
éteindre ay-tañdr	to switch off
les dessins animés lay deh-sañ a-nee-may	cartoons

Where is the television?	**Où est la télévision?** oo ay la tay-lay-vee-zyoñ?
How do you switch it on?	**Comment la met-on en marche?** ko-mahñ la meh toñ ahñ marsh?
What is on television?	**Qu'est-ce qu'il y a à la télé?** kes keel ya a la tay-lay?
When is the news?	**Les informations sont à quelle heure?** lay zañ-for-ma-syoñ soñ ta kel ur?
Do you have any English-language channels?	**Est-ce qu'il y a des chaînes en anglais?** es keel ya day shen ahñ nahñ-gleh?

| Do you have any English videos? | **Avez-vous des vidéos en anglais?** |
| | a-vay voo day vee-day-o ahñ nahñ-gleh? |

Sport

. . . .

Where can I/we...?	**Où est-ce qu'on peut...?**
	oo es koñ puh...?
play tennis	**jouer au tennis**
	zhoo-ay oh teh-nees
play golf	**jouer au golf**
	zhoo-ay oh golf
go swimming	**faire de la natation**
	fehr duh la na-ta-syoñ
go jogging	**faire du jogging**
	fehr dew jo-geeng
How much is it per hour?	**C'est combien l'heure?**
	say koñ-byañ lur?
Do you have to be a member?	**Est-ce qu'il faut être membre?**
	es keel foh (t)etr mahñbr?
Can we hire...?	**Est-ce qu'on peut louer...?**
	es koñ puh loo-ay...?
rackets	**des raquettes**
	day ra-ket

golf clubs	**des clubs de golf**
	day club duh golf
We'd like to go to see (name of team) play	**Nous voudrions aller voir jouer l'équipe de...**
	noo voo-dryoñ a-lay vwar zhoo-ay lay-keep duh...
Where can I/we get tickets?	**Où est-ce qu'on peut avoir des billets?**
	oo es koñ puh a-vwar day bee-yeh?
What sports do you play?	**Qu'est-ce que vous faites comme sports?**
	kes kuh voo fet kom spor?

YOU MAY HEAR...

Il n'y a plus de billets pour le match	There are no tickets left for the game
eel nya plew duh bee-yeh poor luh match	

Skiing

Leisure

débutant day-bew-tahñ	**beginner** (male)
débutante day-bew-tahñt	**beginner** (female)
intermédiaire añ-tehr-may-dyehr	**intermediate**
avancé(e) a-vahñ-say	**advanced**
le ski de fond luh skee duh foñ	**cross-country skiing**
le ski de piste luh skee duh peest	**downhill skiing**

I would like to hire skis	**Je voudrais louer des skis** zhuh voo-dreh loo-ay day skee
Are poles included in the price?	**Est-ce que les bâtons sont compris dans le prix?** es kuh lay ba-toñ soñ koñ-pree dahñ luh pree?
Can you adjust my bindings, please?	**Pourriez-vous régler mes fixations, s'il vous plaît?** poo-ree-ay voo ray-glay may feek-sa-syoñ, seel voo pleh?
How much is a pass for...?	**C'est combien le forfait pour...?** say koñ-byañ luh for-feh poor...?
a day	**une journée** ewn zhoor-nay

a week	**une semaine**
	ewn suh-men
When does the last chair-lift go up?	**À quelle heure part la dernière benne?**
	a kel ur par la dehr-nyehr ben?

YOU MAY HEAR...

Vous avez déjà fait du ski? voo za-vay day-zha feh dew skee?	Have you ever skied before?
Quelle pointure faites-vous? kel pwañ-tewr fet voo?	What is your shoe size?
Quelle longueur de skis voulez-vous? kel loñ gur duh skee voo-lay voo?	What length skis do you want?

Walking

●●

Are there any guided walks?
Y a-t-il des promenades guidées?
ee ya-teel day prom-nad gee-day?

Do you have a guide to local walks?
Avez-vous un guide des promenades dans la région?
a-vay vooz uñ geed day prom-nad dahñ la ray-zhyoñ?

Do you know any good walks?
Vous connaissez de bonnes promenades?
voo ko-neh-say duh bon prom-nad?

How many kilometres is the walk?
La promenade fait combien de kilomètres?
la prom-nad feh koñ-byañ duh kee-lo-metr?

How long will it take?
Ça prendra combien de temps?
sa prahñ-dra koñ-byañ duh tahñ?

Is it very steep?
Est-ce que ça monte dur?
es kuh sa moñt dewr?

We'd like to go climbing
Nous aimerions faire de l'escalade
noo zeh-muh-ryoñ fehr duh les-ka-lad

> **Maps and guides** (p 65)

Leisure

Communications

Telephone and mobile

● ●

The international code for France is **oo 33** plus
the French number you require, without the first
o of the area code. Other international codes are:
Belgium – **oo 32**, Luxembourg – **oo 352**,
Switzerland – **oo 41**. To phone the UK from France,
dial **oo 44** plus the UK area code without the first **o**.
Always dial the area code before the number in
France, even for local calls.

I'd like to make a phone call	**Je voudrais téléphoner** zhuh voo-dreh tay-lay-fo-nay
Is there a pay phone?	**Il y a un téléphone public?** eel ya uñ tay-lay-fon pew-bleek?
A phonecard, please	**Une télécarte, s'il vous plaît** ewn tay-lay-kart, seel voo pleh
for ... euros	**de ... euros** duh ... uh-roh
Do you have a mobile?	**Vous avez un portable?** voo za-vay uñ por-tabl?

What's your mobile number?	**Quel est le numéro de votre portable?**
	kel eh luh new-may-ro duh votr por-tabl?
Can I use your mobile?	**Je peux emprunter votre portable?**
	zhuh puh ahñ-pruñ-tay votr por-tabl?
My mobile number is...	**Le numéro de mon portable est...**
	luh new-may-ro duh moñ por-tabl ay luh...
Monsieur Brun, please	**Monsieur Brun, s'il vous plaît**
	muh-syuh bruñ, seel voo pleh
Extension...	**le poste...**
	luh post...

FACE TO FACE

A **Âllo?**
alo?
Hello

B **Bonjour. Je voudrais parler à..., s'il vous plaît**
boñ-zhoor, zhuh voo-dreh par-lay a..., seel voo pleh
Hello, I'd like to speak to..., please

A **C'est de la part de qui?**
say duh la par duh kee?
Who's calling?

B **De la part de...**
duh la par duh...
This is...

A **Un instant, s'il vous plaît...**
uñ nañ-stahñ seel voo pleh...
Just a moment...

Can I speak to...?	**Pourrais-je parler à...?**	
	poo-rezh par-lay a ...?	
It's (your name)	**... à l'appareil**	
	... a la-pa-ray	
How do I get an outside line?	**Comment on fait pour avoir une ligne extérieure?**	
	ko-mahñ oñ feh poor a-vwar ewn leen-yuh ek-stay-ree-ur?	
I'll call back...	**Je vous rappellerai...**	
	zhuh voo ra-pel-ray...	
later	**plus tard**	
	plew tar	
tomorrow	**demain**	
	duh-mañ	

Je vous le/la passe zhuh voo luh/la pas	I'm putting you through
C'est occupé say to-kew-pay	It's engaged
Pouvez-vous rappeler plus tard? poo-vay voo ra-play plew tar?	Please try later?
Voulez-vous laisser un message? voo-lay voo leh-say uñ meh-sazh?	Do you want to leave a message?
Veuillez laisser votre message après le bip sonore vuh-yay lay-say votr meh-sazh a-preh luh beep so-nor	Please leave a message after the tone
S'il vous plaît, éteignez votre portable seel voo pleh, ay-ten-yay votr por-tabl	Please turn your mobile off

Communications

Text messaging

I will text you	**Je t'enverrai un message** zhuh tahñ-veh-ray uñ meh-sazh
Can you text me?	**Tu peux m'envoyer un message?** tew puh mahñ-vwa-yay uñ meh-sazh?

E-mail

An informal way of starting an e-mail is **Salut**... (Hi...) and ending it **À bientôt** (Speak to you soon). In more formal e-mails to people you know well, begin either **Cher**... (for a man) or **Chère**... (for a woman) and end with **Amicalement**. In formal and business e-mails, begin **Bonjour**... and end **Cordialement**.

New message:	**Nouveau message:**
To:	**A:**
From:	**De:**
Subject:	**Objet:**
CC:	**CC:**
Attachment:	**Pièce jointe:**
Send:	**Envoyer:**

Do you have an e-mail address?	**Vous avez une adresse e-mail?**
	voo za-vay ewn a-dres ee-mehl?
What's your e-mail address?	**Quelle est votre adresse e-mail?**
	kel ay votr a-dres ee-mehl?
How do you spell it?	**Comment ça s'écrit?**
	ko-mahñ sa say-kree?
All one word	**En un seul mot**
	ahñ uñ suhl moh
All lower case	**Tout en minuscules**
	too tahñ mee-new-skewl
My e-mail address is...	**Mon adresse e-mail est...**
	moñ nad-res ee-mehl ay...
caroline.smith@ (company name) .co.uk	**caroline point smith arobase ... point CO point UK**
	ka-roh-leen pwañ smeet a-roh-baz ... pwañ say oh pwañ ew ka
Can I send an e-mail?	**Je peux envoyer un e-mail?**
	zhuh puh ahñ-vwa-yay uñ nee-mehl?
Did you get my e-mail?	**Est-ce que vous avez reçu mon e-mail?**
	es-kuh voo za-vay ruh-sew moñ nee-mehl?

Internet

• •

accueil a-kuh-yuh	home
nom d'utilisateur noñ dew-tee-lee-za-tur	username
moteur de recherche mo-tur duh ruh-shehrsh	search engine
mot de passe moh duh pas	password
contactez-nous koñ-tak-tay-noo	contact us
retour vers le sommaire ruh-toor vehr luh som-mehr	back to menu

Are there any internet cafés here?	**Est-ce qu'il y a des cyber-cafés par ici?** es keel ya day see-behr-ka-fay par ee-see?
How much is it to log on for an hour?	**Combien coûte une heure de connection?** koñ-byañ koot ewn ur duh ko-nek-syoñ?
I can't log on	**Je n'arrive pas à me connecter** zhuh na-reev pa a muh ko-nek-tay

Internet

Fax

• •

Addressing a fax

À/De	To/From
Objet :	Re:
Nombre de pages	Number of pages
Veuillez trouver ci-joint...	Please find attached...

Do you have a fax?	**Avez-vous un fax?**
	a-vay voo uñ fax?
I want to send a fax	**Je voudrais envoyer un fax**
	zhuh voo-dreh ahñ-vwa-yay uñ fax
What is your fax number?	**Quel est votre numéro de fax?**
	kel ay votr new-may-roh duh fax?
My fax number is...	**Mon numéro de fax est le...**
	moñ new-may-roh duh fax ay luh...

Practicalities

Money

....

Banks are generally open from 9 am to 4.30 pm
Monday to Friday, but as closing times vary you are
best advised to go in the morning.

distributeur dees-tree-bew-tur	cash dispenser
retrait espèces ruh-treh es-pes	cash withdrawal

Where can I change some money?	**Où est-ce que je peux changer de l'argent?** oo es kuh zhuh puh shahñ-zhay duh lar-zhahñ?
I want to change these traveller's cheques	**Je voudrais changer ces chèques de voyage** zhuh voo-dreh shahñ-zhay say shek duh vwa-yazh
When does the bank open?	**La banque ouvre quand?** la bahñk oovr kahñ?

When does the bank close?	**La banque ferme quand?**
	la bahñk fehrm kahñ?
Can I pay with pounds/euros?	**Je peux payer en livres sterling/en euros?**
	zhuh puh pay-yay ahñ leevr stehr-leeng/ahñ nuh-roh?
Can I use my credit card with this cash dispenser?	**Je peux utiliser ma carte (de crédit) dans ce distributeur?**
	zhuh puh ew-tee-lee-zay ma kart (duh kray-dee) dahñ suh dee-stree-bew-tur?
Do you have any change?	**Vous avez de la monnaie?**
	voo za-vay duh la mo-neh?

Paying

. . . .

l'addition la-dee-syoñ	**bill** (restaurant)
la note la not	**bill** (hotel)
la facture la fak-tewr	**invoice**
la caisse la kes	**cash desk**

How much is it?	**C'est combien?/Ça fait combien?**
	say koñ-byañ/sa feh koñ-byañ?
How much will it be?	**Ça fera combien?**
	sa fuh-ra koñ-byañ?

Can I pay...?	**Je peux payer...?**
	zhuh puh pay-yay...?
by credit card	**par carte de crédit**
	par kart duh kray-dee
by cheque	**par chèque**
	par shek
Put it on my bill	**Mettez-le sur ma note**
(hotel)	meh-tay luh sewr ma not
The bill, please	**L'addition, s'il vous plaît**
(restaurant)	la-dee-syoñ seel voo pleh
Where do I pay?	**Où doit-on payer?**
	oo dwa-toñ pay-yay?
Do you take	**Vous acceptez les cartes**
credit cards?	**de crédit?**
	voo zak-sep-tay lay kart duh?
	kray-dee?
Is service	**Le service est compris?**
included?	luh sehr-vees ay koñ-pree?
Could you give	**Pourriez-vous me donner**
me a receipt,	**un reçu, s'il vous plaît?**
please?	poo-ree-ay voo muh do-nay uñ
	ruh-sew, seel voo pleh?
Do I pay in	**Est-ce qu'il faut payer à**
advance?	**l'avance?**
	es keel foh pay-yay a la-vahñs?
I'm sorry	**Je suis désolé(e)**
	zhuh swee day-zo-lay
I've nothing	**Je n'ai pas de monnaie**
smaller	zhuh nay pa duh mo-neh
(no change)	

91

Luggage

le retrait de bagages luh ruh-treh duh ba-gazh	baggage reclaim
la consigne la koñ-see-nyuh	left luggage
le chariot à bagages luh sha-ryoh a ba-gazh	luggage trolley

My luggage hasn't arrived yet **Mes bagages ne sont pas encore arrivés** may ba-gazh nuh soñ pa ahñ-kor a-ree-vay

My suitcase has been damaged on the flight **Ma valise a été abîmée pendant le vol** ma va-leez a ay-tay a-bee-may pahñ-dahñ luh vol

Repairs

....

le cordonnier luh kor-don-yay	shoe repairer
réparations minute ray-pa-ra-syoñ mee-newt	repairs while you wait

This is broken | **C'est cassé**
say ka-say
Where can I get this repaired? | **Où est-ce que je peux le faire réparer?**
oo es kuh zhuh puh luh fehr ray-pa-ray?
Can you repair...? | **Pouvez-vous réparer...?**
poo-vay voo ray-pa-ray...?
these shoes | **ces chaussures**
say shoh-sewr
my watch | **ma montre**
ma moñtr

> **Breakdown** (p 45)

Laundry

le pressing luh preh-seeng	dry-cleaner's
la laverie automatique la lav-ree oh-to-ma-teek	launderette
la lessive en poudre la leh-seev ahñ poodr	washing powder

Where can I do some washing?	**Où est-ce que je peux faire un peu de lessive?** oo es kuh zhuh puh fehr uñ puh duh leh-seev?
Is there ... near here?	**Il y a ... près d'ici?** eel ya ... preh dee-see?
a launderette	**une laverie automatique** ewn lav-ree oh-toh-ma-teek
a dry-cleaner's	**un pressing** uñ preh-seeng

Complaints

. . . .

This doesn't work	**Ça ne marche pas**	
	sa nuh marsh pa	
It's dirty	**C'est sale**	
	say sal	
The ... doesn't work	**Le/La ... ne marche pas**	
	luh/la ... nuh marsh pa	
The ... don't work	**Les ... ne marchent pas**	
	lay ... nuh marsh pa	
light	**la lumière**	
	la lew-myehr	
lock	**la serrure**	
	la seh-rewr	
heating	**le chauffage**	
	luh shoh-fazh	
air conditioning	**la climatisation**	
	la klee-ma-tee-za-syoñ	
It's broken	**C'est cassé**	
	say ka-say	
I want a refund	**Je veux être remboursé(e)**	
	zhuh vuh etr rahñ-boor-say	

> **Hotel desk** (p 53)

Problems

Can you help me?	**Pouvez-vous m'aider?**
	poo-vay voo meh-day?
I speak very little French	**Je parle très peu le français**
	zhuh parl treh puh luh frahñ-seh
Does anyone here speak English?	**Est-ce qu'il y a quelqu'un qui parle anglais ici?**
	es keel ya kel-kuñ kee parl ahñ-gleh ee-see?
I would like to speak to whoever is in charge	**Je voudrais parler au responsable**
	zhuh voo-dreh par-lay oh reh-spoñ-sabl
I'm lost	**Je me suis perdu(e)**
	zhuh muh swee pehr-dew
How do I get to...?	**pour aller à/au...?**
	poor a-lay a/oh...?
I missed...	**J'ai raté...**
	zhay ra-tay...
my train	**mon train**
	moñ trañ
my plane	**mon avion**
	moñ na-vyoñ
my connection	**ma correspondance**
	ma ko-res-poñ-dahñs

Practicalities

I've missed my flight because there was a strike	**J'ai raté mon avion à cause d'une grève** zhay ra-tay moñ na-vyoñ a kohz dewn grev
The coach has left without me	**Le car est parti sans moi** luh kar ay par-tee sahñ mwa
Can you show me how this works?	**Pouvez-vous me montrer comment ça marche?** poo-vay voo muh moñ-tray ko-mahñ sa marsh?
I have lost my purse	**J'ai perdu mon porte-monnaie** zhay pehr-dew moñ port-mo-neh
I need to get to...	**Je dois aller à/au (etc.)...** zhuh dwa a-lay a/oh...
Leave me alone!	**Laissez-moi tranquil(le)!** leh-say mwa trahñ-keel!
Go away!	**Allez-vous en!** a-lay voo zahñ!

97

Emergencies

....

police po-lees	police
ambulance ahñ-bew-lahñs	ambulance
pompiers poñ-pyay	fire brigade
commissariat ko-mee-sar-ya	police station (in large towns)
gendarmerie zhahñ-darm-ree	police station (in villages and small towns)
urgences ewr-zhahñs	accident and emergency department

Help!	**Au secours!** oh skoor!
Fire!	**Au feu!** oh fuh!
Can you help me?	**Pouvez-vous m'aider?** poo-vay voo meh-day?
There has been an accident	**Il y a eu un accident** eel ya ew uñ nak-see-dahñ
Someone has been injured	**Il y a un blessé** eel ya uñ bleh-say
He/she has been knocked down by a car	**Il/elle a été renversé(e) par une voiture** eel/el a ay-tay rahñ-vehr-say par ewn vwa-tewr
Please call...	**S'il vous plaît, appelez...** seel voo pleh, a-puh-lay...

the police	**la police** la po-lees
an ambulance	**une ambulance** ewn ahñ-bew-lahñs
Where is the police station?	**Où est le commissariat?** oo eh luh ko-mee-sar-ya?
I want to report a theft	**Je veux signaler un vol** zhuh vuh seen-ya-lay uñ vol
I've been robbed/ attacked	**On m'a volé/attaqué(e)** oñ ma vo-lay/a-ta-kay
I've been raped	**On m'a violée** oñ ma vee-o-lay
I want to speak to a policewoman	**Je veux parler à une femme agent de police** zhuh vuh par-lay a ewn fam a-zhahñ duh po-lees
Someone has stolen...	**On m'a volé...** oñ ma vo-lay...
my handbag	**mon sac à main** moñ sak a mañ
my money	**mon argent** moñ nar-zhahñ
My car has been broken into	**On a forcé ma voiture** oñ na for-say ma vwa-tewr
My car has been stolen	**On m'a volé ma voiture** oñ ma vo-lay ma vwa-tewr
I need to make a telephone call	**Il faut que je passe un coup de téléphone** eel foh kuh zhuh pas uñ koo duh tay-lay-fon

I need a report for my insurance	**Il me faut un constat pour mon assurance**
	eel muh foh uñ kon-sta poor moñ na-sew-rahñs
I didn't know the speed limit	**Je ne savais pas quelle était la limite de vitesse**
	zhuh nuh sa-veh pa kel ay-teh la lee-meet duh vee-tes
How much is the fine?	**C'est une amende de combien?**
	say tewn a-mahñd duh koñ-byañ?
Where do I pay it?	**Où dois-je la payer?**
	oo dwa-zhuh la pay-yay?
Do I have to pay it straight away?	**Est-ce qu'il faut la payer immédiatement?**
	es keel foh la pay-yay ee-may-dyat-mahñ?
I'm very sorry, officer	**Je suis vraiment désolé(e), monsieur l'agent**
	zhuh swee vray-mahñ day-zo-lay, muh-syuh la-zhahñ

YOU MAY HEAR...

Vous avez brûlé un feu rouge voo za-vay brew-lay uñ fuh roozh	You went through a red light
Vous n'avez pas cédé la priorité voo na-vay pa say-day la pree-o-ree-tay	You didn't give way

Health

Pharmacy

la pharmacie la far-ma-see	pharmacy/chemist's
la pharmacie de garde la far-ma-see duh gard	duty chemist's

Can you give me something for...?	**Avez-vous quelque chose pour le/la (etc.)...?** a-vay voo kel-kuh shohz poor luh/la...?
a headache	**le mal de tête** luh mal duh tet
car sickness	**le mal des transports** luh mal day trahñ-spor
flu	**la grippe** la greep
diarrhoea	**la diarrhée** la dya-ray
sunburn	**les coups de soleil** lay koo duh so-leh-yuh

Is it safe for children?	**C'est sans danger pour les enfants?**
	say sahñ dahñ-zhay poor lay zahñ-fahñ?
How much should I give him/her?	**Combien je dois lui en donner?**
	koñ-byañ zhuh dwa lwee ahñ do-nay?

YOU MAY HEAR...

Prenez-en trois fois par jour avant/pendant/ après le repas	Take it three times a day before/with/ after meals
pruh-nay zahñ trwa fwa par zhoor avahñ/pahñ-dahñ/ a-preh luh ruh-pa	

Doctor

• •

In French the possessive (my, his, her, etc.) is generally not used with parts of the body, e.g.

I've broken my leg	**Je me suis cassé(e) la jambe**
He has hurt his ankle	**Il s'est fait mal à la cheville**

hôpital o-pee-tal	hospital
urgences ewr-zhahñs	accident and emergency department
consultations koñ-sewl-ta-syoñ	surgery hours

FACE TO FACE

A **Je me sens mal**
zhuh muh sahñ mal
I feel ill

B **Vous avez de la fièvre?**
voo za-vay duh la fyehvr?
Do you have a temperature?

A **Non, J'ai mal ici**
noñ, zhay mal ee-see
No, I have a pain here

I need a doctor	**J'ai besoin d'un médecin** zhay buh-zwañ duñ may-dsañ
My son/My daughter is ill	**Mon fils/Ma fille est malade** moñ fees/ma fee ay ma-lad
I'm diabetic	**Je suis diabétique** zhuh swee dya-bay-teek
I'm pregnant	**Je suis enceinte** zhuh swee ahñ-sañt

Doctor

103

I'm on the pill	**Je prends la pilule**
	zhuh prahñ la pee-lewl
I'm allergic to penicillin	**Je suis allergique à la pénicilline**
	zhuh swee za-lehr-zheek a la pay-nee-see-leen
Will she/he have to go to hospital?	**Faut-il la/le transporter à l'hôpital?**
	foh-teel la/luh trahñ-spor-tay a lo-pee-tal?
Will I have to pay?	**Est-ce que je dois payer?**
	es kuh zhuh dwa pay-yay?
How much will it cost?	**Combien ça va coûter?**
	koñ-byañ sa va koo-tay?
I need a receipt for the insurance	**Il me faut un reçu pour l'assurance**
	eel muh foh uñ ruh-sew poor la-sew-rahñs

YOU MAY HEAR...

Il faut que vous alliez à l'hôpital eel foh kuh voo zal-yay a lo-pee-tal	You will have to go to hospital
Ce n'est pas très grave suh nay pa treh grav	It's not serious

Health

> **Emergencies** (p 98)

Dentist

....

I need to see a dentist	**J'ai besoin de voir un dentiste**
	zhay buh-zwañ duh vwar uñ dahñ-teest
He/She has toothache	**Il/Elle a mal aux dents**
	eel/el a mal oh dahñ
Can you do a temporary filling?	**Pouvez-vous me faire un plombage momentané?**
	poo-vay voo muh fehr uñ ploñ-bazh mo-mahñ-ta-nay?
Can you give me something for the pain?	**Pouvez-vous me donner quelque chose contre la douleur?**
	poo-vay voo muh do-nay kel-kuh shohz koñtr la doo-lur?
It hurts	**Ça me fait mal**
	sa muh feh mal
Can you repair my dentures?	**Pouvez-vous me réparer mon dentier?**
	poo-vay voo muh ray-pa-ray moñ dahñt-yay?
Do I have to pay?	**Je dois payer?**
	zhuh dwa pay-yay?
How much will it be?	**Combien ça va coûter?**
	koñ-byañ sa va koo-tay?

I need a receipt for my insurance	**Il me faut un reçu pour mon assurance**
	eel muh foh uñ ruh-sew poor moñ na-sew-rahñs

Il faut l'arracher eel foh la-ra-shay	It has to come out
Il faut faire un plombage eel foh fehr uñ ploñ-bazh	You need a filling

Health

106

Different types of travellers

Disabled travellers

What facilities do you have for disabled people?	**Qu'est-ce que vous avez comme aménagements pour les handicapés?** kes kuh voo za-vay kom a-may-nazh-mahñ poor lay zahñ-dee-ka-pay?
Are there any toilets for the disabled?	**Est-ce qu'il y a des toilettes pour handicapés?** es keel ya day twa-let poor ahñ-dee-ka-pay?
Do you have any bedrooms on the ground floor?	**Avez-vous des chambres au rez-de-chaussée?** a-vay voo day shahñbr oh ray duh shoh-say?
Is there a lift?	**Est-ce qu'il y a un ascenseur?** es keel ya uñ na-sahñ-sur?
Where is the lift?	**Où est l'ascenseur?** oo eh la-sahñ-sur?

Do you have wheelchairs?	**Est-ce qu'il y a des fauteuils roulants?**
	es keel ya day foh-tuh-yuh roo-lahñ?
Can you visit ... in a wheelchair?	**On peut visiter ... en fauteuil roulant?**
	oñ puh vee-zee-tay ... ahñ foh-tuh-yuh roo-lahñ?
Do you have an induction loop?	**Est-ce que vous avez une boucle pour mal-entendants?**
	es kuh voo za-vay ewñ bookl poor mal-ahñ-tahñ-dahñ?
Is there a reduction for disabled people?	**Est-ce qu'il y a une réduction pour les handicapés?**
	es keel ya ewn ray-dewk-syoñ poor lay zahñ-dee-ka-pay?
Is there somewhere I can sit down?	**Est-ce qu'il y a un endroit où on peut s'asseoir?**
	es keel ya uñ nahñ-drwa oo oñ puh sa-swar?

> **Hotel** (p 50)

With kids

Public transport is free for children under four.
Children between four and twelve pay half price.

A child's ticket	**Un billet tarif enfant** un bee-yeh ta-reef ahñ-fahñ
He/She is ... years old	**Il/Elle a ... ans** eel/el a ... ahñ
Is there a reduction for children?	**Est-ce qu'il y a une réduction pour les enfants?** es keel ya ewn ray-dewk-syoñ poor lay zahñ-fahñ?
Do you have a children's menu?	**Est-ce que vous avez un menu enfant?** es kuh voo za-vay uñ muh-new poor ahñ-fahñ?
Is it OK to take children?	**On peut y aller avec des enfants?** on puh ee a-lay a-vek day zahñ-fahñ?
Do you have...?	**Avez-vous...?** a-vay voo...?
a high chair	**une chaise de bébé** ewn shez duh bay-bay
a cot	**un lit d'enfant** uñ lee dahñ-fahñ

I have two children	**J'ai deux enfants**
	zhay duh zahñ-fahñ
He/She is 10 years old	**Il/Elle a dix ans**
	eel/el a dee zahñ
Do you have any children?	**Est-ce que vous avez des enfants?**
	es kuh voo za-vay day zahñ-fahñ?

Different types of travellers

> **Pharmacy** (p 101) > **Doctor** (p 102)

Reference

Alphabet

. . . .

The French alphabet is the same as the English alphabet. Below are the words used for clarification when spelling something out.

Comment ça s'écrit? ko-mahñ sa say-kree?	How do you spell it?
A comme Anatole, B comme Berthe a kom a-na-tol, bay kom behrt	A for Anatole, B for Berthe

A	a	**Anatole**	a-na-tol
B	bay	**Berthe**	behrt
C	say	**Célestin**	say-les-tañ
D	day	**Désiré**	day-zee-ray
E	uh	**Eugène**	uh-zhen
F	ef	**François**	frahñ-swa
G	zhay	**Gaston**	gas-toñ
H	ash	**Henri**	ahñ-ree
I	ee	**Irma**	eer-ma

Alphabet

J	zhee	**Joseph**	zho-zef
K	ka	**Kléber**	klay-behr
L	el	**Louis**	loo-wee
M	em	**Marcel**	mar-sel
N	en	**Nicolas**	nee-koh-la
O	oh	**Oscar**	os-kar
P	pay	**Pierre**	pyehr
Q	kew	**Quintal**	kañ-tal
R	ehr	**Raoul**	ra-ool
S	es	**Suzanne**	sew-zan
T	tay	**Thérèse**	tay-rez
U	ew	**Ursule**	ewr-sewl
V	vay	**Victor**	veek-tor
W	doo-bluh-vay	**William**	weel-yam
X	eex	**Xavier**	za-vyay
Y	ee-grek	**Yvonne**	ee-von
Z	zed	**Zoé**	zoh-ay

Reference

Measurements and quantities

• •

1 lb = approx. 0.5 kilo   1 pint = approx. 0.5 litre

Liquids

1/2 litre of...	**un demi-litre de...** uñ duh-mee leetr duh...
a litre of...	**un litre de...** uñ leetr duh...
1/2 bottle of...	**une demi-bouteille de...** ewn duh-mee-boo-tay-yuh duh...
a bottle of...	**une bouteille de...** ewn boo-tay-yuh duh...
a glass of...	**un verre de...** uñ vehr duh...

Weights

100 grams of...	**cent grammes de...** sahñ gram duh...
1/2 kilo of...	**un demi-kilo de...** uñ duh-mee kee-loh duh...
a kilo of...	**un kilo de...** uñ kee-loh duh...

Food

a slice of...	**une tranche de...**
	ewn trahñsh duh...
a portion of...	**une portion de...**
	ewn por-syoñ de...
a dozen...	**une douzaine de...**
	ewn doo-zen duh...
a box of...	**une boîte de...**
	ewn bwat duh...
a packet of...	**un paquet de...**
	uñ pa-keh duh...
a tin of...	**une boîte de...**
	ewn bwat duh...
a carton of...	**une brique de...**
	ewn breek duh...
a jar of...	**un pot de...**
	uñ poh duh...

Miscellaneous

500 euros of...	**500 euros de...**
	sañk uh-roh duh...
a quarter	**un quart**
	uñ kar
ten per cent	**dix pour cent**
	dee poor sahñ
more...	**plus de...**
	plew duh...

Reference

less...	**moins de...**
	mwañ duh...
enough of...	**assez de...**
	a-say duh...
double	**le double**
	luh doobl
twice	**deux fois**
	duh fwa

Numbers

. . . .

0	**zéro** zay-roh
1	**un** uñ
2	**deux** duh
3	**trois** trwa
4	**quatre** katr
5	**cinq** sañk
6	**six** sees
7	**sept** set
8	**huit** weet
9	**neuf** nuhf
10	**dix** dees
11	**onze** oñz
12	**douze** dooz
13	**treize** trez
14	**quatorze** ka-torz
15	**quinze** kañz

16	**seize** scz	
17	**dix-sept** dees-set	
18	**dix-huit** deez-weet	
19	**dix-neuf** deez-nuhf	
20	**vingt** vañ	
21	**vingt et un** vañ tay uñ	
22	**vingt-deux** vañt-duh	
23	**vingt-trois** vañt-trwa	
30	**trente** trahñt	
40	**quarante** ka-rahñt	
50	**cinquante** sañk-ahñt	
60	**soixante** swa-sahñt	
70	**soixante-dix** swa-sahñt-dees	
71	**soixante et onze** swa-sahñt-ay-oñz	
72	**soixante-douze** swa-sahñt-dooz	
80	**quatre-vingts** katr-vañ	
81	**quatre-vingt-un** katr-vañ-un	
82	**quatre-vingt-deux** katr-vañ-duh	
90	**quatre-vingt-dix** katr-vañ-dees	
91	**quatre-vingt-onze** katr-vañ-oñz	
100	**cent** sahñ	
110	**cent dix** sahñ dees	
200	**deux cents** duh sahñ	
250	**deux cent cinquante** duh sahñ sañk-ahñt	
1,000	**mille** meel	
1 million	**un million** uñ mee-lyoñ	

Days and months

1st	**premier/première/**	pruh-myay/
	1er/1ère	pruh-myehr
2nd	**deuxième/2e**	duh-zyem
3rd	**troisième/3e**	trwa-zyem
4th	**quatrième/4e**	kat-ree-yem
5th	**cinquième/5e**	sañk-yem
6th	**sixième/6e**	see-zyem
7th	**septième/7e**	set-yem
8th	**huitième/8e**	wee-tyem
9th	**neuvième/9e**	nuh-vyem
10th	**dixième/10e**	dee-zyem

Days

Monday	**lundi**	luñ-dee
Tuesday	**mardi**	mar-dee
Wednesday	**mercredi**	mehr-kruh-dee
Thursday	**jeudi**	zhuh-dee
Friday	**vendredi**	vahñ-druh-dee
Saturday	**samedi**	sam-dee
Sunday	**dimanche**	dee-mahñsh

Months

January	**janvier**	zhahñ-vyay
February	**février**	fay-vree-yay
March	**mars**	mars
April	**avril**	av-reel
May	**mai**	meh
June	**juin**	zhwañ
July	**juillet**	zhwee-yeh
August	**août**	oo(t)
September	**septembre**	sep-tahñbr
October	**octobre**	ok-tobr
November	**novembre**	no-vahñbr
December	**décembre**	day-sahñbr

Seasons

spring	**printemps**	prañ-tahñ
summer	**été**	ay-tay
autumn	**automne**	oh-ton
winter	**hiver**	ee-vehr

What is today's date?	**Quelle est la date aujourd'hui?** kel eh la dat oh-zhoor-dwee?
It's the fifth of March	**Nous sommes le cinq mars** noo som luh sañk mars

It's 8th May 2007	**C'est le huit mai deux mille sept**
	say luh wee may duh meel set
1st January	**Le premier janvier**
	luh pruhm-yay zhahñ-vyay
on Saturday	**samedi**
	sam-dee
on Saturdays	**le samedi**
	luh sam-dee
every Saturday	**tous les samedis**
	too lay sam-dee
this Saturday	**samedi qui vient**
	sam-dee kee vyañ
next Saturday	**samedi prochain**
	sam-dee pro-shañ
last Saturday in June	**samedi dernier en juin**
	sam-dee dehr-nyay ahñ zhwañ
at the beginning of June	**début juin**
	day-bew zhwañ
at the end of June	**fin juin**
	fañ zhwañ
before the summer	**avant l'été**
	a-vahñ lay-tay
during the summer	**pendant l'été**
	pahñ-dahñ lay-tay
after the summer	**après l'été**
	a-preh lay-tay

Time

•••••••••••••••••••••••••••••••

The 24-hour clock is used a lot more in Europe than in Britain. After 1200 (midday), it continues: 13.00 (**treize heures** – one o'clock in the afternoon), 14.00 (**quatorze heures** – two o'clock), 15.00 (**quinze heures** – three o'clock), etc. until 24.00 (**vingt-quatre heures** – midnight). With the 24-hour clock, the words **quart** (quarter) and **demie** (half) aren't used:

13.15 (1.15 pm)	**treize heures quinze**
19.30 (7.30 pm)	**dix-neuf heures trente**
22.45 (10.45 pm)	**vingt-deux heures quarante-cinq**
What time is it?	**Il est quelle heure?/**
	Quelle heure est-il?
	eel ay kel ur?/kel ur ay-teel?
It's...	**Il est...**
	eel ay...
one o'clock	**deux heures**
	duh zur
two o'clock	**trois heures**
	trwa zur
six o'clock (etc.)	**six heures**
	see zur

It's one o'clock	**Il est une heure**	
	eel ay (t)ewn ur	
It's midday	**Il est midi**	
	eel ay mee-dee	
It's midnight	**Il est minuit**	
	eel ay mee-nwee	
9	**neuf heures**	
	nuh vur	
9.10	**neuf heures dix**	
	nuh vur dees	
quarter past 9	**neuf heures et quart**	
	nuh vur ay kar	
9.20	**neuf heures vingt**	
	nuh vur vañ	
9.30	**neuf heures et demie/**	
	neuf heures trente	
	nuh vur ay duh-mee/	
	nuh vur trahñt	
9.35	**dix heures moins vingt-cinq**	
	dee zur mwañ vañt-sañk	
quarter to 10	**dix heures moins le quart**	
	dee zur mwañ luh kar	
10 to 10	**dix heures moins dix**	
	dee zur mwañ dees	

Time phrases

●●●●●●●●●●●●●●●●●●●●●●●●●●●●●●●●●●

When does it...?	**Il ... à quelle heure?**
	eel ... a kel ur?
open/close/ begin/finish	**ouvre/ferme/commence/ finit**
	oovr/fehrm/ko-mahñs/fee-nee
at three o'clock	**à trois heures**
	a trwa zur
before three o'clock	**avant trois heures**
	a-vahñ trwa zur
after three o'clock	**après trois heures**
	a-preh trwa zur
today	**aujourd'hui**
	oh-zhoor-dwee
tonight	**ce soir**
	suh swar
tomorrow	**demain**
	duh-mañ
yesterday	**hier**
	ee-yehr

Eating out

Eating places

Salon de thé Generally attached to a cake shop, **pâtisserie**, where you can sit down and sample some of the cakes. Can be quite expensive.

Crêperie Specialising in sweet and savoury pancakes (**galettes**). Good for light inexpensive meals.

Libre-service Self-service.

Bistro Usually cheaper and smaller than **Brasserie**.

Glacier Ice-cream parlour.

Restaurant Generally open 11.30 am to 2.30 pm and 7.30 to 10.30 pm. The menu is posted outside.

Table d'hôte Home cooking using local produce.

Brasserie All-day food place often attached to a **bar-café**.

Frites 500m Signals a road-side café 500 metres away. Mediocre food (mostly chips).

Gaufres Waffles.

In a bar/café

If you just ask for **un café** you will be served a small, strong, black coffee. If this is not your cup of tea, you should specify the type of coffee you want:

un (café) crème uñ (ka-fay) krem	white creamy coffee
un grand crème uñ grahñ krem	large white creamy coffee
un café au lait uñ ka-fay oh leh	coffee with hot milk

a coffee	**un café** uñ ka-fay
an orangeade	**une orangeade** ewn o-rahñ-zhad

A Qu'est-ce que vous prenez?
kes kuh voo pruh-nay?
What will you have?

B Un thé au lait, s'il vous plaît
uñ tay oh leh, seel voo pleh
A tea with milk, please

with lemon	au citron
	oh see-troñ
no sugar	sans sucre
	sahñ sewkr
for two	pour deux personnes
	poor duh pehr-son
for me	pour moi
	poor mwa
for him/her	pour lui/elle
	poor lwee/el
for us	pour nous
	poor noo
with ice, please	avec des glaçons, s'il vous plaît
	a-vek day gla-soñ, seel voo pleh
Some ... mineral water	De l'eau minérale...
	duh loh mee-nay-ral...
sparkling	gazeuse
	ga-zuhz
still	plate
	plat

In a bar/café

Other drinks to try

un chocolat (chaud) hot chocolate
un citron pressé freshly-squeezed lemon
  (add water and sugar)
un diabolo lemonade and cordial
une tisane herb tea

Reading the menu

Restaurants display their menus outside. Often
there is a choice of two or three menus at different
prices as well as **à la carte** dishes. French families
often go to a restaurant for Sunday lunch, so it is
advisable to book.

Boisson non comprise Drink not included.

**Plat du jour à 7 € 50 – poisson ou viande ou
  vollaille garnis** Dish of the day 7 € 50 - fish or
  meat or poultry with veg and French fries.

menu du midi – entrée + plat + café lunchtime
  menu – starter + main course + coffee.

carte	menu
entrées	starters
potages	soups
assiette de charcuterie	assorted cold meats
assiette de crudités	assorted raw veg & dip
viandes	meat
gibier et volaile	game & poultry
poissons	fish
fruit de mer	seafood
légumes	vegetables
fromages	cheese
desserts	desserts
boissons	drinks

In a restaurant

FACE TO FACE

A **Je voudrais réserver une table pour ... personnes**
zhuh voo-dreh ray-zehr-vay ewn tabl poor ... pehr-son
I'd like to book a table for ... people

Oui, pour quand?
B wee, poor kahñ?
Yes, when for?

A **Pour ce soir/pour demain soir/pour dix-neuf
heures trente**
poor suh swar/poor duh-mañ swar/poor deez-nuh
vur trahñt
For tonight/for tomorrow night/for 7.30

The menu, please	**Le menu, s'il vous plaît** luh muh-new, seel voo pleh
What is the dish of the day?	**Quel est le plat du jour?** kel eh luh pla dew zhoor?
I'll have the menu at ... euros, please	**Je prends le menu à ... euros, s'il vous plaît** zhuh prahñ luh muh-new a ... uh-roh, seel voo pleh
Can you recommend a local dish?	**Pouvez-vous nous recommander un plat régional?** poo-vay voo noo ruh-ko-mahñ-day uñ pla ray-zhyo-nal?

What is in this?	**Qu'est-ce qu'il y a dedans?**
	kes keel ya duh-dahñ?
I'll have this	**Je prends ça**
	zhuh prahñ sa
More bread...	**Encore du pain...**
	ahñ-kor dew pañ...
More water...	**Encore de l'eau...**
	ahñ-kor duh loh...
please	**s'il vous plaît**
	seel voo pleh
The bill, please	**L'addition, s'il vous plaît**
	la-dee-syoñ, seel voo pleh
Is service included?	**Est-ce que le service est compris?**
	es kuh luh sehr-vees ay koñ-pree?

YOU MAY HEAR...

| **Une table pour deux?** | A table for two? |
| ewn tabl poor duh? | |

Vegetarian

Don't expect great things if you're a vegetarian (let alone a vegan) – the French love meat!

Are there any vegetarian restaurants here?	**Est-ce qu'il y a des restaurants végétariens ici?** es keel ya day res-toh-rahñ vay-zhay-ta-ryañ ee-see?
Do you have any vegetarian dishes?	**Vous avez des plats végétariens?** voo za-vay day pla vay-zhay-ta-ryañ?
Which dishes have no meat/fish?	**Quels sont les plats sans viande/poisson?** kel soñ lay plah sahñ vyahñd/pwasoñ?
I'd like pasta as a main course	**Je voudrais des pâtes comme plat principal** zhuh voo-dreh day pat kom pla prañ-see-pal
I don't like meat	**Je n'aime pas la viande** zhuh nehm pa la vyahñd
Is it made with vegetable stock?	**Est-ce que c'est fait avec du bouillon de légumes?** es kuh say feh a-vek dew boo-yoñ duh lay-gewm?

Possible dishes

salade verte green salad

salade niçoise salad with tomatoes, olives, tuna and eggs

artichauts à la sauce fromage artichokes in cheese sauce

soupe à l'oignon French onion soup

tarte à l'oignon onion tart

ratatouille courgettes, tomatoes, peppers, onions and aubergines

Wines and spirits

The wine list, please	**La carte des vins, s'il vous plaît** la kart day vañ, seel voo pleh
white wine/ red wine	**du vin blanc/du vin rouge** dew vañ blahñ/dew vañ roozh
Can you recommend a good wine?	**Pouvez-vous nous recommander un bon vin?** poo-vay voo noo ruh-ko-mahñ-day uñ boñ vañ?
A bottle...	**Une bouteille...** ewn boo-tay-yuh...
A carafe...	**Un pichet...** uñ pee-sheh...
of the house wine	**de la cuvée du patron** duh la kew-vay dew pa-troñ

Wines

Barsac sweet white wine

Beaujolais light, fruity wines (Burgundy)

Bergerac red and white wines (Dordogne)

Blanc de blancs any white wine made from white grapes only

Blanquette de Limoux dry sparkling white wine (southwest)

Bordeaux region producing red (claret), rosé and dry and sweet white wines

Bourgueil light, fruity red wine to be drunk very young (Loire)

Brouilly among the finest Beaujolais: fruity, supple, full of flavour

Cabernet sauvignon red wine with a slight blackcurrant aroma

Cahors dark, long-lived, powerful red wine from the southwest

Chablis very dry, full-bodied white wine (Burgundy)

Chambertin one of the finest red Burgundies (Burgundy)

Champagne sparkling white/rosé (Champagne)

Chardonnay a white grape variety widely used in sparkling wines

Châteauneuf-du-Pape good, full-bodied red wine (Rhône)

Côtes de Beaune full-bodied red (Burgundy)

Côtes du Rhône full-bodied red (Rhône)

Côtes du Roussillon good ordinary red
  (Languedoc-Roussillon)
Entre-deux-mers medium-dry white wine from
  Bordeaux
Gewürztraminer fruity, spicy white wine (Alsace)
Mâcon good ordinary red and white wines (Burgundy)
Médoc principal wine-producing area of Bordeaux
Mersault high-class dry white wine (Burgundy)
Monbazillac sweet white wine (Dordogne)
Muscadet very dry white wine (Loire)
Pouilly-fuissé light dry white wine (Burgundy)
Pouilly-fumé spicy dry white wine (Loire)
Rosé d'Anjou light, fruity rosé (Loire)
Saint-Emilion good full-bodied red wine (Bordeaux)
Sancerre dry white wine (Loire)
Sauternes high-class sweet white wine (Bordeaux)
Sylvaner dry white wine (Alsace)
Vouvray dry, sweet and sparkling white wines (Loire)

Demi-sec medium dry (wine)
Cuvée vintage
Mousseux sparkling (wine)
Premier cru first-class wine

Spirits and liqueurs

What liqueurs do you have?	**Qu'est-ce que vous avez comme digestifs?**
	kes kuh voo za-vay kom dee-zheh-steef?

Armagnac fine grape brandy from southwest France

Calvados apple brandy made from cider (Normandy)

Cassis blackcurrant liqueur: *kir* white wine and cassis apéritif

Chartreuse aromatic herb liqueur made by Carthusian monks

Cognac high-quality white grape brandy

Cointreau orange-flavoured liqueur

Crème de menthe peppermint-flavoured liqueur

Eau de vie very strong brandy (often made from plum, pear, etc.)

Grand Marnier tawny-coloured, orange-flavoured liqueur

Kirsch cherry-flavoured spirit from Alsace

Marc white grape spirit

Mirabelle plum spirit from Alsace

Pastis aniseed-based apéritif (e.g. Pernod) to which water is added

Menu reader

à la/à l'/au/aux... in the style of.../with...

abats offal, giblets

abricot apricot

agneau lamb

ail garlic

aile wing

aïoli rich garlic mayonnaise served on the side and giving its name to the dish it accompanies: cold steamed fish and vegetables

airelles bilberries, cranberries

allumettes very thin chips

amande almond

amuse-bouche nibbles

armoricaine, à l' cooked with brandy, wine, tomatoes and onions

ananas pineapple

anchoïade anchovy paste usually served on grilled French bread

anchois anchovies

andouille (eaten cold), andouillette (eaten hot) spicy tripe sausage

anguille eel

anis aniseed

arachide peanut (uncooked)
araignée de mer spider crab
artichaut artichoke
asperge asparagus
aspic de volaille chicken in aspic
assiette dish, platter
　assiette anglaise plate of assorted cold meats
　assiette de charcuterie plate of assorted pâtés
　and salami
　assiette de crudités selection of raw vegetables
　assiette du pêcheur assorted fish or seafood
aubergine aubergine
avocat avocado

babas au rhum rum baba
Badoit mineral water, very slightly sparkling
baekenofe hotpot of pork, mutton and beef baked
　in white wine with potato layers (from Alsace)
bar sea-bass
barbue brill
barquette small boat-shaped flan
basilic basil
bavarois moulded cream and custard pudding,
　usually served with fruit
Béarnaise, à la sauce similar to mayonnaise
　but flavoured with tarragon and white wine –
　traditionally served with steak
bécasse woodcock
beignets fritters, doughnuts

betterave beetroot
beurre butter
  beurre blanc, au sauce of white wine and shallots
  with butter
bien cuit well done
bière beer
  (bière) pression draught beer
  bière blonde lager
  bière brune bitter
bifteck steak
bigorneau periwinkle
bio(logique) organic
bis wholemeal (of bread or flour)
biscuit de Savoie sponge cake
bisque smooth, rich seafood soup
blanquette white meat stew served with a creamy
  white sauce
  blanquette de veau veal stew in white sauce
  blanquette de volaille chicken stew in white sauce
blé wheat
blette Swiss chard
bleu very rare
bœuf beef
  bœuf bourguignon beef in burgundy, onions and
  mushrooms
  bœuf en daube rich beef stew with wine, olives,
  tomatoes and herbs
bombe moulded ice cream dessert
bonite bonito, small tuna fish

bouchée vol-au-vent
  bouchée à la reine vol-au-vent filled with chicken or veal and mushrooms in a white sauce
boudin pudding made with offal and blood
bouillabaisse rich seafood dish flavoured with saffron originally from Marseilles
bouilli boiled
bouillon stock
boulettes meatballs
brandade de morue dried salt cod puréed with potatoes and olive oil
brème bream
brioche sweet bun
  brioche aux fruits sweet bun with glacé fruit
brochet pike
brochette kebab
  brochette, en cooked like a kebab (on a skewer)
brugnon nectarine
bugnes doughnuts from the Lyons area
bulot whelk

cabillaud fresh cod
cacahuète peanut
café coffee
  café au lait coffee with hot milk
caille quail
cajou, noix de cashew nut
calisson almond dessert
calmar/calamar squid

canard duck
  canard périgourdin roast duck with prunes, **pâté de foie gras** and truffles
caneton duckling
cannelle cinnamon
câpres capers
carbonnade de bœuf braised beef
cardon cardoon
cari curry
carottes Vichy carrots cooked in butter and sugar
carpe farcie carp stuffed with mushrooms or **foie gras**
carrelet plaice
carte des vins wine list
cassoulet bean stew with pork or mutton, confit and sausages (there are many regional variations)
caviar blanc mullet roe
  caviar niçois a paste made with anchovies and olive oil
céleri rémoulade celeriac in a mustard and herb dressing
céleri-rave celeriac
cèpes boletus mushrooms, wild mushrooms
cerfeuil chervil
cerise cherry
cervelas smoked pork sausages, saveloy
cervelle brains (usually lamb or calf)
  cervelle de Canut savoury dish of fromage frais, goat's cheese, herbs and white wine

champignon mushroom

  champignons à la grecque mushrooms cooked in wine, olive oil, herbs and tomato

  champignons de Paris button mushrooms

chantilly whipped cream

charlotte custard and fruit in lining of almond fingers

chasseur literally hunter-style, cooked with white wine, shallots, mushrooms and herbs

châtaigne chestnut

châteaubriand thick fillet steak

chaud(e) hot

chauffé(e) heated

chausson pasty filled with meat or seafood

  chausson aux pommes apple turnover

chèvre goat

chevreuil venison

chichi doughnut shaped as a stick

chicorée chicory, endive

chocolat chaud hot chocolate

chou cabbage

choucroute sauerkraut

  choucroute garnie sauerkraut with various types of sausages

chou-fleur cauliflower

choux brocolis broccoli

choux de Bruxelles Brussels sprouts

ciboule/cive spring onions

ciboulette chives

cidre cider, sparkling (**bouché**) or still, quite strong

citron lemon

  citron pressé freshly squeezed lemon juice with water and sugar

citron vert lime

citrouille pumpkin

civet thick stew

  civet de langouste crayfish in wine sauce

  civet de lièvre hare stewed in wine, onions and mushrooms

clafoutis cherry pudding

clou de girofle clove

cochon pig

coco coconut

cœur heart

  cœurs d'artichauts artichoke hearts

  cœurs de palmier palm hearts

coing quince

colin hake

compote de fruits mixed stewed fruit

concombre cucumber

condé rich rice pudding with fruits

confit pieces of meat preserved in fat

  confit de canard/d'oie duck/goose meat preserved in its own fat

confiture jam

  confiture d'oranges marmalade

congre conger eel

consommé clear soup, generally made from meat or fish stock

contre-filet sirloin fillet (beef)

coq au vin chicken and mushrooms cooked in red wine

coquelet cockerel

coques cockles

coquillages shellfish

coquilles Saint-Jacques scallops

coquillettes pasta shells

cornichon gherkin

côtelettes d'agneau lamb cutlets

côtes de porc pork chops

cotriade fish stew (Brittany)

cou neck

coulibiac salmon cooked in puff pastry

coulis puréed fruit sauce

coupe goblet with ice cream

courge marrow

crabe crab

craquelots smoked herring

crémant sparkling wine

crème cream

   crème anglaise fresh custard

   crème au beurre butter cream with egg yolks and sugar

   crème chantilly slightly sweetened whipped cream

   crème pâtissière thick fresh custard used in tarts and desserts

   crème renversée (or **crème caramel**) custard with a caramelised top

crème de cream of... (soup)

crème d'Argenteuil white asparagus soup
crème de cresson watercress soup
crème de marrons chestnut purée
crêpes sweet and savoury pancakes
crêpes fourrées filled pancakes
crêpes Suzette pancakes with a Cointreau or Grand Marnier sauce usually flambéed
crevette prawn
crevette grise shrimp
crevette rose large prawn
croque-madame grilled cheese and bacon, sausage, chicken or egg sandwich
croque-monsieur grilled gruyère cheese and ham sandwich
croûte, en in pastry
croûtes/croûtons, aux served with croutons (cubes of toasted or fried bread)
cru(e) raw
crudités assortment of raw vegetables (grated carrots, sliced tomatoes, etc.) served as a starter
crustacés shellfish
cuisses de grenouille frogs' legs
cuit cooked
culotte rump steak

darne fish steak
datte date
daube casserole with wine, herbs, garlic, tomatoes and olives

dauphinoise, à la baked in milk
daurade sea bream
diabolo menthe mint cordial and lemonade
dinde turkey

eau water
  eau de Seltz soda water
  eau-de-vie brandy (often made from plum, pear, etc)
  eau minérale mineral water
  eau du robinet tap water
échalote shallot
échine loin of pork
écrevisse freshwater crayfish
églefin haddock
encornet squid
endive chicory
entrecôte rib steak
entrées starters
entremets desserts
épaule shoulder
éperlan whitebait
épice spice
épinards spinach
escargots snails (generally cooked with strong seasonings)
espadon swordfish
estouffade de boeuf beef stew cooked in red
  wine, herbs, onions, mushrooms and diced bacon
estragon tarragon
esturgeon sturgeon

faisan pheasant
farci(e) stuffed
faux-filet sirloin steak
fenouil fennel
feu de bois, au cooked over a wood fire
feuille leaf
feuilleté(e) in puff pastry
fèves broad beans
figue fig
filet fillet steak
  filet de bœuf en croûte steak in pastry
  filet de bœuf tenderloin
  filet mignon small pork fillet steak
fine de claire high-quality oyster
fines herbes mixed, chopped herbs
flageolet type of small green haricot bean
flétan halibut
flocons d'avoine oat flakes
florentine with spinach, usually served with
  mornay sauce
foie liver (usually calf's)
  foie de volailles chicken livers
foie gras goose liver
fond d'artichaut artichoke heart
fondue (au fromage) melted cheeses with white
  wine into which chunks of bread are dipped
fondue bourguignonne small chunks of beef
  dipped into boiling oil and eaten with different
  sauces

fougasse type of bread with various fillings (olives, anchovies)

four, au baked

fourré(e) stuffed

frais (fraîche) fresh

fraise strawberry

  fraises des bois wild strawberries

framboise raspberry

frappé iced

fricassée a stew, usually chicken or veal, and vegetables

frisée curly endive

frit(e) fried

friture fried food, usually small fish

froid(e) cold

fromage cheese

  fromage blanc soft white cheese

  fromage frais creamy fresh cheese

froment wheat

fruit de la passion passion fruit

  fruits de mer shellfish, seafood

fumé(e) smoked

fumet fish stock

galantine meat in aspic

galette savoury buckwheat pancake

gambas large prawn

ganache chocolate cream filling

garni(e) garnished i.e. served with something, usually vegetables

garnitures side dishes

gâteau cake, gateau

  gâteau Saint-Honoré choux pastry cake filled with custard

gaufres waffles (often cream-filled)

gazeuse sparkling

gelée jelly, aspic

genièvre juniper berry

génoise sponge cake

germes de soja bean sprouts

gésier gizzard

gibier game

gigot d'agneau leg of lamb

gigot de mer large fish baked whole

gingembre ginger

glace ice cream

gougères choux pastry with cheese

goyave guava

gratin, au topped with cheese and breadcrumb and grilled

gratin dauphinois potatoes cooked in cream, garlic and Swiss cheese

grecque, à la cooked in olive oil, garlic, tomatoes and herbs, can be served hot or cold

grenade pomegranate

grenouilles frogs' legs

  grenouilles meunière frogs' legs cooked in butter and parsley

grillade grilled meat

groseille redcurrant
groseille à maquereau gooseberry

hachis mince
hareng herring
haricots beans
  haricots beurre butter beans
  haricots blancs haricot beans
  haricots rouges red kidney beans
  haricots verts green beans, French beans
herbes (fines herbes) herbs
hollandaise, sauce sauce made of butter, egg
  yolks and lemon juice, served warm
homard lobster
  homard à l'armoricaine lobster cooked with
  onions, tomatoes and wine
hors d'œuvre variés selection of appetizers
huile oil
  huile d'arachide groundnut oil
  huile de tournesol sunflower oil
huître oyster

îles flottantes soft meringues floating on fresh
  custard

jambon ham
  jambon de Bayonne cured raw ham from the
  Basque country
  jambon de Paris boiled ham

julienne with vegetables cut into fine strips
jus juice, meat-based glaze or sauce

lait milk
  lait (demi)-écrémé (semi)-skimmed milk
  lait entier full-cream milk
laitue lettuce
lamproie à la bordelaise lamprey in red wine
langouste crayfish (saltwater)
langoustines scampi (large)
langue tongue (veal, beef)
lapin rabbit
lard fat, streaky bacon
lardon strip of fat, diced bacon
laurier bayleaf
légumes vegetables
levure yeast
lièvre hare
limande lemon sole
lotte monkfish
loup de mer sea-bass

macaron macaroon
macédoine (de fruits) fresh fruit salad
macédoine de légumes mixed cooked vegetables
madeleine small sponge cake
magret de canard duck breast
maïs/maïs doux maize, sweetcorn
mangue mango

maquereau mackerel

marcassin young wild boar

marinière, à la in a sauce of white wine, onions and herbs (mussels or clams)

marjolaine marjoram

marron chestnut

  marrons glacés candied chestnuts

  marrons Mont Blanc chestnut purée and cream

matelote fresh-fish stew

médaillon thick, medal-sized slice of meat

menthe mint

merguez spicy red sausage

merlan whiting

merluche hake

mérou grouper

merveilles fritters flavoured with brandy

mignonnette small fillet of lamb

mijoté(e) stewed

mille-feuille thin layers of pastry filled with custard

mirabelle small yellow plum; plum brandy from Alsace

mont-blanc pudding made with chestnuts and cream

Mornay, sauce béchamel and cheese sauce

morue dried salt cod

moules mussels

  moules marinière mussels cooked in white wine

  moules poulette mussels in wine, cream and mushroom sauce

mousseline mashed potatoes with cream and eggs

moutarde mustard
mouton mutton or sheep
mûre blackberry
muscade nutmeg
myrtille bilberry

navet turnip
noisette hazelnut
noisettes d'agneau small round pieces of lamb
noix walnut; general term for a nut
nouilles noodles
œuf egg
  œufs à la coque soft-boiled eggs
  œufs au plat fried eggs
  œufs brouillés scrambled eggs
  œufs durs hard-boiled eggs
  œufs en cocotte eggs baked in individual
  containers with wine
  œufs frits fried eggs and bacon
oie goose
oignon onion
omelette nature plain omelette
omelette norvégienne baked Alaska
onglet cut of beef (steak)
orge barley
os bone
oseille sorrel
oursin sea urchin

pain bread, loaf of bread

  pain au chocolat croissant with chocolate filling

  pain bagnat bread roll with egg, olives, salad, tuna, anchovies and olive oil

  pain bis brown bread

  pain complet wholemeal bread

  pain d'épices ginger cake

  pain de mie white sliced loaf

  pain de seigle rye bread

  pain grillé toast

palmier caramelized puff pastry

palombe wood pigeon

palourde clam

pamplemousse grapefruit

panais parsnip

pané(e) with breadcrumbs

panisse thick chickpea flour pancake

papillote, en in filo pastry

parfait rich home-made ice cream

Paris Brest ring-shaped cake filled with praline-flavoured cream

parisienne, à la sautéed in butter with white wine, sauce and shallots

parmentier with potatoes

pastèque watermelon

patate douce sweet potato

pâté de foie de volailles chicken liver pâté

  pâté en croûte pâté encased in pastry

pâtes pasta
paupiettes meat slices stuffed and rolled
pavé thick slice
pêche peach
perche perch (fish)
perdreau/perdrix partridge, grouse
Périgueux, sauce with truffles
persil parsley
persillé(e) with parsley
pétillant(e) fizzy
petit-beurre butter biscuit
petits farcis stuffed tomatoes, aubergines,
  courgettes and peppers
petits fours bite-sized cakes and pastries
petit pain roll
petits pois small peas
petit-suisse thick fromage frais
pieds et paquets mutton or pork tripe and trotters
pignons pine nuts
pilon drumstick (chicken)
piment chilli
  piment doux sweet pepper
  piment fort chilli
pimenté(e) peppery, hot
pintade/pintadeau guinea fowl
pipérade tomato, pepper and onion omelette
piquant(e) spicy
pissaladière a kind of pizza made mainly in the Nice
  region, filled with onions, anchovies and black olives

pistache pistachio

pistou garlic, basil and olive oil sauce from Provence – similar to **pesto**

plat dish

  plat (principal) main course

plat(e) still (e.g. water)

plie plaice

poché(e) poached

poêlé(e) pan-fried

pimenté(e) peppery, hot

point, à medium rare

poires belle Hélène poached pears with vanilla ice cream and chocolate sauce

poireau leek

pois peas

  pois cassés split peas

pois-chiches chickpeas

poisson fish

poitrine breast (lamb or veal)

poivre pepper

poivron sweet pepper

  poivron rouge red pepper

  poivron vert green pepper

pomme apple

pomme (de terre) potato

  pommes à l'anglaise boiled potatoes

  pommes à la vapeur steamed potatoes

  pommes allumettes match-stick chips

  pommes dauphine potato croquettes

pommes duchesse potato mashed then baked in the oven

pommes frites fried potatoes

pommes Lyonnaise potatoes fried with onions

pommes mousseline potatoes mashed with cream

pommes rissolées small deep-fried potatoes

porc pork

pot au feu beef and vegetable stew

potage soup, generally creamed or thickened

potée auvergnate cabbage and meat soup

potiron type of pumpkin

poularde fattened chicken

poulet chicken

poulet basquaise chicken stew with tomatoes, mushrooms and peppers

poulet célestine chicken cooked in white wine with mushrooms and onion

poulpe à la niçoise octopus in tomato sauce

pousses de soja bean sprouts

poussin baby chicken

poutargue mullet roe paste

praire clam

praliné hazelnut-flavoured

primeurs spring vegetables

provençale, à la cooked with tomatoes, peppers, garlic and white wine

pruneau prune, damson

purée mashed potatoes; purée

quatre-quarts cake made with equal parts of butter, flour, sugar and eggs

quenelles poached balls of fish or meat mousse served in a sauce

  quenelles de brochet pike mousse in cream sauce

queue de bœuf oxtail

râble saddle

radis radishes

ragoût stew, casserole

raie skate

raifort horseradish

raisin grape

raisin sec sultana, raisin

raïto red wine, olive, caper, garlic and shallot sauce

ramier wood pigeon

râpé(e) grated

rascasse scorpion fish

ratatouille tomatoes, aubergines, courgettes and garlic cooked in olive oil

rave turnip

reine-claude greengage

rillettes coarse pork pâté

  rillettes de canard coarse duck pâté

ris de veau calf sweetbread

riz rice

rognon kidney

rognons blancs testicles

romaine cos lettuce

romarin rosemary
rond de gigot lamb leg steak
rosbif roast beef
rôti(e) roast
rouget red mullet
rouille spicy version of garlic mayonnaise (**aïoli**)
  served with fish stew or soup
roulade meat or fish, stuffed and rolled
roulé sweet or savoury roll
rutabaga swede

sabayon dessert made with egg yolks, sugar and
  Marsala wine
sablé shortbread
safran saffron
saignant rare
Saint-Hubert game consommé flavoured with wine
salade lettuce; salad
  salade de fruits fruit salad
  salade de saison mixed salad and/or greens in
  season
  salade lyonnaise vegetable salad (cooked),
  dressed with eggs, bacon and croutons
  salade niçoise many variations on a famous
  theme: the basic ingredients are green beans,
  anchovies, black olives and green peppers
  salade russe mixed cooked vegetables in mayonnaise
  salade verte green salad
salé(e) salted/spicy

salsifis salsify, oyster plant (root vegetable resembling asparagus and palm hearts)

sanglier wild boar

sarrasin buckwheat

sarriette savoury (herb)

sauce piquante gherkins, vinegar and shallots

saucisse/saucisson sausage

saumon salmon

  saumon fumé smoked salmon

  saumon poché poached salmon

sauté(e) sautéed

sauté d'agneau lamb stew

savarin a filled ring-shaped cake

savoyarde, à la with gruyère cheese

sec dry, dried

seiche cuttlefish

sel salt

selle d'agneau saddle of lamb

semoule semolina

sole cardinal sole cooked in wine, served with lobster sauce

  sole Normande sole cooked in a cream, cider and shrimp sauce

  sole Saint Germain grilled sole with butter and tarragon sauce

sole-limande lemon sole

soufflé au Grand Marnier soufflé flavoured with Grand Marnier liqueur

  soufflé au jambon ham soufflé

soupe hearty and chunky soup

  soupe à l'oignon onion soup usually served with a crisp chunk of French bread in the dish with grated cheese piled on top

  soupe au pistou vegetable soup with garlic and basil

  soupe aux choux cabbage soup with pork

steak steak

  stea(c)k au poivre steak with peppercorns

  stea(c)k tartare minced raw steak mixed with raw egg, chopped onion, tartare or worcester sauce, parsley and capers

sucre sugar

sucré(e) sweet

suprême de volaille breast of chicken in cream sauce

tapenade olive paste

tarte open tart, generally sweet

  tarte flambée thin pizza-like pastry topped with onion, cream and bacon (Alsace)

  tarte Normande apple tart

  tarte tatin upside down tart with caramelized apples or pears

  tarte tropézienne sponge cake filled with custard cream and topped with almonds

tartine open sandwich

terrine terrine, pâté

  terrine de campagne pork and liver terrine

  terrine de porc et gibier pork and game terrine

tête de veau calf's head

thé tea

  thé au citron tea with lemon

  thé au lait tea with milk

  thé sans sucre tea without sugar

thermidor lobster grilled in its shell with cream
  sauce

thon tuna fish

tilleul lime tea

timbale round dish in which a mixture of meat or
  fish is cooked – often lined with pastry and served
  with a rich sauce

  timbale d'écrevisses crayfish in a cream, wine
  and brandy sauce

  timbale de fruits pastry base covered with fruits

tomate tomato

  tomates à la provençale grilled tomatoes
  steeped in garlic

tomme type of cheese

tournedos thick fillet steak

tourte à la viande meat pie usually made with
  veal and pork

tripes à la mode de Caen tripe cooked with
  vegetables, herbs, cider and calvados

tripoux mutton tripe

truffe truffle

truite aux amandes trout covered with almonds

vacherin large meringue filled with cream,
  ice cream and fruit

vapeur, **à la** steamed
veau calf, veal
  veau sauté Marengo veal cooked in a casserole
  with white wine, garlic, tomatoes and mushrooms
velouté thick creamy white sauce made with fish,
  veal or chicken stock – also used in soups
venaison venison
verdure, **en** garnished with green vegetables
verjus juice of unripe grapes
verveine herbal tea made with verbena
viande meat
viande séchée thin slices of cured beef
vichyssoise leek and potato soup, served cold
vin wine
  vin blanc white wine
  vin de pays local regional wine
  vin de table table wine
  vin rosé rosé wine
  vin rouge red wine
vinaigre vinegar
violet sea squirt
volaille poultry

yaourt yoghurt

Grammar

Nouns

. . . .

Unlike English nouns, French nouns have a gender: they are either masculine (**le**) or feminine (**la**). Therefore words for *the* and *a(n)* must agree with the noun they accompany. Like English nouns, they can be singular or plural, but the plural words for *the* (**les**) and *some* (**des**) are the same in both masculine and feminine:

	masculine	feminine	plural
the	**le chat**	**la rue**	**les chats/ rues**
a, an	**un chat**	**une rue**	**des chats/ rues**

If the noun begins with a vowel (*a, e, i, o* or *u*) or, sometimes, an *h*, **le** and **la** shorten to **l'**, e.g. **l'avion** (*m*), **l'école** (*f*), **l'hôtel** (*m*). The letter *h* is never sounded in French and, unfortunately, there is no rule for distinguishing which words beginning with *h* take **l'** and which **le/la**.

Note: **le** and **les** used after the prepositions **à** (to, at)
and **de** (any, some, of) contract as follows:

à + **le** = **au** (**au cinéma** but **à la gare**)
à + **les** = **aux** (**aux magasins** – applies to both
            m and *f*)
de + **le** = **du** (**du pain** but **de la confiture**)
de + **les** = **des** (**des pommes** – applies to both
            m and *f*)

Plurals

The general rule is to add an **s** to the singular:

  le chat → **les chats**

Exceptions occur with the following noun endings:
-**eau**, -**eu**, -**al**

  le bateau → **les bateaux**
  le neveu → **les neveux**
  le cheval → **les chevaux**

Nouns ending in **s**, **x**, or **z** do not change in the plural.

  le dos → **les dos**
  le prix → **les prix**
  le nez → **les nez**

Adjectives

• •

Adjectives normally follow the noun they describe in French, e.g:

la pomme <u>verte</u> → (the <u>green</u> apple)

French adjectives have to reflect the gender of the noun they describe. To make an adjective feminine, an **e** is added to the masculine form (where this does not already end in an **e**, e.g. **jeune**). A final consonant, which is usually silent in the masculine form, is pronounced in the feminine:

masc.	fem.
le livre vert (the green book) luh leevr vehr	**la pomme verte** (the green apple) la pom vehrt

To make an adjective plural, an **s** is added to the singular form: masculine plural – **verts** (remember the ending is still silent: vehr) or feminine plural – **vertes** (because of the **s**, the **t** is sounded: vehrt).

My, your, his, her, their...

These words also depend on the gender and number of the noun they accompany and not on the sex of the 'owner'.

	with masc. sing. noun	with fem. sing. noun	with plural noun
my	**mon**	**ma**	**mes**
your (familiar sing.)	**ton**	**ta**	**tes**
his/her	**son**	**sa**	**ses**
our	**notre**	**notre**	**nos**
your (polite/pl.)	**votre**	**votre**	**vos**
their	**leur**	**leur**	**leurs**

e.g. **la clé** (key)   **sa clé** (his/her key)
     le passeport   **son passeport**
        (passport)   (his/her passport)
     les billets (tickets) **ses billets**
                                (his/her tickets)

Pronouns

•••

Grammar

subject		object	
I	**je, j'**	me	**me, m'**
you (familiar sing.)	**tu**	you	**te, t'**
you (polite/pl.)	**vous**	you	**vous**
he/it	**il**	him/it	**la, l'**
she/it	**elle**	her/it	**la, l'**
we	**nous**	us	**nous**
they (masc.)	**ils**	them	**les**
they (fem.)	**elles**	them	**les**

In French there are two words for *you* – **tu** and
vous. **Tu** is the familiar form, which is used with
people you know well (friends and family), children
and animals. **Vous**, as well as being the plural form
of *you*, is also the polite way of addressing someone.
You should take care to use this form until the other
person invites you to use the more familiar **tu**.

Object pronouns are placed before the verb, e.g.

    il <u>vous</u> aime   (he loves <u>you</u>)
    nous <u>la</u> connaissons (we know <u>her</u>)

However, in commands or requests, object pronouns follow the verb, e.g.

écoutez-le (listen to <u>him</u>)
aidez-moi (help <u>me</u>)

This does not apply to negative commands or requests, e.g.

ne le faites pas (don't do <u>it</u>)

Verbs

There are three main patterns of endings for verbs in French – those ending **-er**, **-ir** and **-re** in the dictionary.

donner	**to give**
je donne	I give
tu donnes	you give
il/elle donne	he/she gives
nous donnons	we give
vous donnez	you give
ils/elles donnent	they give

finir	**to finish**
je finis	I finish
tu finis	you finish
il/elle finit	he/she finishes
nous finissons	we finish
vous finissez	you finish
ils/elles finissent	they finish

répondre	**to reply**
je réponds	I reply
tu réponds	you reply
il/elle répond	he/she replies
nous répondons	we reply
vous répondez	you reply
ils/elles répondent	they reply

Irregular verbs

Among the most important irregular verbs are the following:

être	**to be**
je suis	I am
tu es	you are
il/elle est	he/she is
nous sommes	we are
vous êtes	you are
ils/elles sont	they are

avoir	**to have**
j'ai	I have
tu as	you have
il/elle a	he/she has
nous avons	we have
vous avez	you have
ils/elles ont	they have
aller	**to go**
je vais	I go
tu vas	you go
il/elle va	he/she goes
nous allons	we go
vous allez	you go
ils/elles vont	they go
pouvoir	**to be able**
je peux	I can
tu peux	you can
il/elle peut	he/she can
nous pouvons	we can
vous pouvez	you can
ils/elles peuvent	they can

Past tense

• •

To form the simple past tense of most verbs, e.g.
I finished/I have finished, combine the present tense
of the verb **avoir** (to have) with the past participle of
the verb (**donné**, **fini**, **répondu**), e.g.

j'ai donné	I gave/I have given
j'ai fini	I finished/I have finished
j'ai répondu	I replied/I have replied

Not all verbs take **avoir** as their auxiliary verb; some
verbs take **être** (**je suis**..., **il est**..., etc.). These are
intransitive verbs (which have no object), e.g.

je suis allé	I went
je suis né	I was born

When the auxiliary verb **être** is used, the past
participle (**allé**, **né**, etc.) becomes adjectival and
agrees with the subject of the verb, e.g.

nous sommes allés	we went *(plural)*
je suis née	I was born *(female)*

Public holidays

●●

In France public holidays are taken on the day on which they fall. Many of the larger shops now open on public holidays, but it is always best to check before you go.

When a public holiday falls on a Tuesday or Thursday, it is common for people to take the Monday or the Friday off as well. This is known as **faire le pont** (making a bridge).

January 1st	**Le Jour de l'An**	New Year's Day
March or April	**Le Lundi de Pâques** Easter Monday	
May 1st	**La Fête du Travail** Labour Day/May Day	
May 8th	**Le huit mai** Victory Day	
April or May (40 days after Easter)	**L'Ascension** Ascension	
May or June (49 days after Easter)	**Le Lundi de Pentecôte** Whit Monday (no longer an official holiday, but many employees are still given the day off)	
July 14th	**La Fête Nationale** Bastille Day	
August 15th	**L'Assomption** Assumption	
November 1st	**La Toussaint** All Saints' Day	
November 11th	**L'Armistice 1918** Armistice Day	
December 25th	**Noël** Christmas Day	

English – French

English	French	Pronunciation
A		
a(n)	un m/une f	uñ/ewn
able: to be able to	pouvoir	poo-vwar
about	vers; environ	vehr; ahñ-vee-roñ
(approximately)		
(concerning)	au sujet de	oh sew-zheh duh (duh)
above	au-dessus (de)	oh duh-sew (duh)
abroad	à l'étranger	a lay-trahñ-zhay
to accept	accepter	ak-sep-tay
access	l'accès m	ak-seh
accident	l'accident m	ak-see-dahñ
accident & emergency department	les urgences	ewr-zhahñs
accommodation	le logement	lozh-mahñ
address	l'adresse f	a-dres
what is the address?	quelle est l'adresse?	kel ay la-dres?
admission charge	l'entrée f	ahñ-tray
adult	l'adulte m/f	a-dewlt
aeroplane	l'avion m	a-vyoñ
after	après	apreh
afternoon	l'après-midi m	a-preh mee-dee
in the afternoon	dans l'après-midi	dahñ la-preh mee-dee
this afternoon	cet après-midi	set a-preh mee-dee
again	encore	ahñkor
against	contre	koñtr
age	l'âge m	azh
ago: a week ago	il y a une semaine	eel ya ewn suh-men
air-conditioning	la climatisation	klee-ma-tee-za-syoñ
airplane	l'avion m	a-vyoñ
airport	l'aéroport m	a-ay-ro-por
airport bus	la navette pour l'aéroport	navet por la-ay-ro-por
alarm	l'alarme f	a-larm
alarm clock	le réveil	ray-vay

alcohol-free	sans alcool	sahñ zal-kol	**antibiotic**	l'antibiotique *m*	ahñ-tee-bee-o-teek
all	tout(e)/tous/toutes	too(t)/toos/toot	**antihistamine**	l'anthista-minique *m*	ahñ-tee-ee-sta-mee-neek
allergic	allergique	a-lehr-zheek	**any**	de(du/de la/des)	duh (dew/duh la/day)
I'm allergic to...	je suis allergique à...	zhuh swee za-lehr-zheek a...	**anything**	quelque chose	kel-kuh shoz
allergy	l'allergie *f*	a-lehr-zhee	**apartment**	l'appartement *m*	a-par-tuh-mahñ
all right (agreed)	d'accord	dakor	**apple**	la pomme	pom
are you all right?	ça va?	sa va?	**appointment**	le rendez-vous	rahñ-day-voo
almost	presque	presk	**approximately**	environ	ahñ-vee-roñ
already	déjà	day-zha	**April**	avril	av-reel
also	aussi	oh-see	**arm**	le bras	bra
always	toujours	too-zhoor	**to arrange**	arranger	a-rahñ-zhay
a.m.	du matin	dew ma-tañ	**arrival**	l'arrivée *f*	a-ree-vay
ambulance	l'ambulance *f*	ahñ-bew-lahñs	**to arrive**	arriver	a-ree-vay
America	l'Amérique *f*	a-may-reek	**to ask**	demander	duh-mahñ-day
American	américain(e)	a-may-ree-kañ/ken	**aspirin**	l'aspirine *f*	as-pee-reen
			asthma	l'asthme *m*	as-muh
and	et	ay	*I have asthma*	je suis asthmatique	zhuh swee zas-ma-teek
another	un(e) autre	uñ/ewn ohtr			

English – French

172|173

English – French

English	French	Pronunciation
at	à	a
at my/your home	chez moi/vous	shay mwa/voo
at 8 o'clock	à huit heures	a weet ur
at night	la nuit	la nwee
August	août	oo(t)
Australia	l'Australie *f*	oh-stra-lee
Australian	australien(ne)	oh-stra-lyañ/lee-en
autumn	l'automne *m*	oh-ton
available	disponible	dees-poh-neebl
B		
baby	le bébé	bay-bay
baby milk (formula)	le lait maternisé	leh ma-tehr-nee-zay
baby's bottle	le biberon	bee-broñ
back (of body)	le dos	doh
backpack	le sac à dos	sak a doh
bad (food, weather)	mauvais(e)	moh-veh/vez
bag	le sac	sak
baggage	les bagages	ba-gazh
bank (money)	la banque	bahñk
bank (river)	la rive; le bord	reev; bor
banknote	le billet de banque	bee-yeh duh bahñk
bar	le bar	bar
bath	le bain	bañ
bathroom	la salle de bains	sal duh bañ
battery (for radio, camera, etc.)	la pile	peel
B&B	la chambre d'hôte	shahñbr doht
to be	être	etr
beach	la plage	plazh
beautiful	beau (belle)	boh (bel)
because	parce que	pars kuh
bed	le lit	lee
double bed	le grand lit; le lit de deux personnes	grahñ lee; lee duh duh pehr-son

single bed	le lit d'une personne	lee dewn pehr-son
twin beds	les lits jumeaux	lee zhew-moh
bedroom	la chambre (à coucher)	shahñbr (a koo-shay)
beer	la bière	byehr
before	avant	a-vahñ
to begin	commencer	koh-mahñ-say
behind	derrière	deh-ree-yehr
to belong to	appartenir à	a-par-tuh-neer a
below	sous	soo
beside (next to)	à côté de	a koh-tay duh
better (than)	meilleur(e) (que)	meh-yur(kuh)
between	entre	ahñtr
bicycle	le vélo	vay-loh
big	grand(e); gros(se)	grahñ(d); groh(s)
bigger (than)	plus grand(e) (que); plus gros(se) (que)	plew grahñ(d) (kuh); plew groh(s) (kuh)

bill (restaurant)	l'addition f	a-dee-syoñ
(hotel)	la note	not
(for work done)	la facture	fak-tewr
bin (dustbin)	la poubelle	poo-bel
bit: *a bit (of)*	un peu (de)	uñ puh (duh)
bite (animal)	la morsure	mor-sewr
(insect)	la piqûre	pee-kewr
black	noir(e)	nwar
blanket	la couverture	koo-vehr-tewr
blind (person)	aveugle	a-vuh-gluh
blocked	bouché(e)	boo-shay
blood	le sang	sahñ
blue	bleu(e)	bluh
to board (plane, train, etc.)	embarquer	ahñ-bar-kay
boarding card	la carte d'embarquement	kart dahñ-bar- kuh mahñ
boat	le bateau	ba-toh
(rowing)	la barque	bark
book	le livre	leevr
to book (reserve)	réserver	ray-sehr-vay

English – French

English – French

booking	la reservation	ray-sehr-va-syoñ
booking office	le bureau de location	bew-roh duh lo-ka-syoñ
bookshop	la librairie	lee-breh-ree
to borrow	emprunter	añ-pruñ-tay
bottle	la bouteille	boo-tay-yuh
boy	le garçon	gar-soñ
boyfriend	le copain	ko-pañ
bread	le pain	pañ
bread roll	le petit pain	puh-tee pañ
breakdown (car)	la panne	pan
breakfast	le petit déjeuner	puh-tee day-zhuh-nay
bridge	le pont	poñ
briefcase	la serviette	sehr-vyet
Britain	la Grande-Bretagne	grahñd-bruh-tan-yuh
British	britannique	bree-ta-neek
broken	cassé(e)	ka-say
my leg is broken	je me suis cassé(e) la jambe	zhuh muh swee ka-say la zhahñb

broken down (car, etc.)	en panne	añ pan
brother	le frère	frehr
brown	marron	ma-roñ
building	l'immeuble *m*	ee-muh-bluh
burger	le hamburger	añ-bewr-gehr
bus (coach)	le bus	bews
	le car	kar
bus station	la gare routière	gar roo-tyehr
bus stop	l'arrêt de bus *m*	a-reh duh bews
bus ticket	le ticket de bus	tee-keh duh bews
busy	occupé(e)	o-kew-pay
but	mais	meh
to buy	acheter	a-shtay
by (via)	par	par
by bus	à côté de	a koh-tay duh
	en bus	añ bews
by car	en voiture	añ wa-tewr
by ship	en bateau	añ ba-toh
by train	en train	añ trañ

C

English	French	Pronunciation
cab (taxi)	le taxi	tak-see
café	le café	ka-fay
internet café	le cybercafé	see-behr-ka-fay
cake (large)	le gâteau	ga-toh
(small)	la pâtisserie; le petit gateau	pa-tee-sree; puh-tee ga-toh
call (telephone)	l'appel *m*	a-pel
to call (speak, phone)	appeler	a-puh-lay
camera	l'appareil photo *m*	a-pa-ray foh-toh
camping gas	le butane	bew-tan
campsite	le camping	kahñ-peeng
can (to be able to)	pouvoir	poo-vwar
(to know how to)	savoir	sa-vwar
I can	je peux/sais	zhuh puh/seh
we can	nous pouvons/ savons	noo poo-voñ/ sa-voñ
can	la boîte	bwat
Canada	le Canada	ka-na-da
Canadian	canadien(ne)	ka-na-dyañ/dyen
to cancel	annuler	a-new-lay
car	la voiture	vwa-tewr
car hire	la location de voitures	lo-ka-syoñ duh vwa-tewr
car insurance	l'assurance automobile *f*	a-sew-rahñs oh-toh-mo-beel
car keys	les clés de voiture	klay duh vwa-tewr
car park	le parking	par-keeng
card	la carte	kart
careful:		
to be careful	faire attention	fehr a-tahñ-syoñ
be careful!	attention!	a-tahñ-syoñ!
carpet (rug)	le tapis	ta-pee
(fitted)	la moquette	mo-ket
carriage (railway)	la voiture	vwa-tewr
case (suitcase)	la valise	va-leez
cash	l'argent liquide *m*	ar-zhahñ lee-keed

English – French

English – French

English	French	pronunciation
cash dispenser (ATM)	le distributeur automatique (de billets)	dee-stree-bew-tur oh-toh-ma-teek (duh bee-yeh)
castle	le château	sha-toh
catch (bus, train)	prendre	prahñdr
cathedral	la cathédrale	ka-tay-dral
Catholic	catholique	ka-toh-leek
cellphone	le (téléphone) portable	(tay-lay-fon) por-tabl
cent (euro)	un centime	uñ sahñ-teem
central	central(e)	sahñ-tral
central heating	le chauffage central	shoh-fazh sahñ-tral
centre	le centre	sahñtr
cereal	la céréale	say-ray-al
chair	la chaise	shez
change (coins)	la monnaie	mo-neh
to change	changer	shahñ-zhay
to change money	changer de l'argent	shahñ-zhay duh ar-zhahñ
to change clothes	se changer	suh shahñ-zhay
to change trains	changer de train	shahñ-zhay duh trañ
Channel (English)	la Manche	mahñsh
charge (fee)	le prix	pree
to charge a phone	recharger un téléphone	ruh-shar-zhay uñ tay-lay-fon
cheap	bon marché	boñ mar-shay
cheaper	moins cher	mwañ shehr
to check	vérifier	vay-ree-fyay
to check in	enregistrer	ahñ-ruh-zhee-stray
check-in (desk) (at hotel)	l'enregistrement	ahñ-ruh-zhees-truh-mahñ
cheers!	la réception	ray-sep-syoñ
chemist's	santé!	sahñ-tay!
cheque	la pharmacie	far-ma-see
child	le chèque	shek
children	l'enfant *m*	ahñ-fahñ
	les enfants	ahñ-fahñ

English	French	
for children	pour enfants	poor ahñ-fahñ
chilli (fruit)	le piment	pee-mahñ
chili con carne	le chili con carne	shee-lee kon kar-nay
chips	les frites	freet
chocolate	le chocolat	sho-ko-la
drinking-chocolate	le chocolat en poudre	sho-ko-la ahñ poodr
hot chocolate	le chocolat chaud	sho-ko-la shoh
chocolates	les chocolats	sho-ko-la
to choose	choisir	shwa-zeer
Christmas	Noël *m*	noh-el
church	l'église *f*	ay-gleez
cigarette	la cigarette	see-ga-ret
cigarette lighter	le briquet	bree-keh
cinema	le cinéma	see-nay-ma
city	la ville	veel
city centre	le centre-ville	sahñtr-veel
clean	propre	propr

English	French	
to clean	nettoyer	neh-twa-yay
clock	l'horloge *f*	or-lozh
close by	proche	prosh
closed (shop, etc.)	fermé(e)	fehr-may
clothes	les vêtements	vet-mahñ
coach (bus)	le car; l'autocar *m*	kar; loh-toh-kar
coast	la côte	koht
coat	le manteau	mahñ-toh
coffee	le café	ka-fay
white coffee	le café au lait	ka-fay oh leh
black coffee	le café noir	ka-fay nwar
cappuccino	le cappuccino	ka-pew-chee-noh
decaffeinated coffee	le café décaféiné/déca	ka-fay-ee-nay/day-ka
coin	la pièce de monnaie	pyes duh mo-neh
Coke®	le Coca®	ko-ka
cold	froid(e)	frwa(d)
I'm cold	j'ai froid	zhay frwa

English – French

English – French

English	French	Pronunciation
it's cold	il fait froid	eel feh fwa
cold (illness)	le rhume	rewm
I have a cold	j'ai un rhume	zhay uñ rewm
to come	venir	vuh-neer
(to arrive)	arriver	a-ree-vay
to come back	revenir	ruh-vuh-neer
to come in	entrer	ahñ-tray
come in!	entrez!	ahñ-tray!
comfortable	confortable	coñ-for-tabl
company (firm)	la compagnie; la société	koñ-pa-nyee; so-syay-tay
to complain	faire une réclamation	fehr ewn ray-kla-ma-syoñ
complaint	la plainte	plañt
compulsory	obligatoire	ob-lee-ga-twar
computer	l'ordinateur *m*	or-dee-na-tur
concert	le concert	koñ-sehr
concession	la réduction	ray-dewk-syoñ
conference	la conférence	koñ-fay-rahñs
to confirm	confirmer	koñ-feer-may
confirmation	la confirmation	koñ-feer-ma-syoñ
consulate	le consulat	koñ-sew-la
contact lenses	les verres de contact	vehr duh koñ-takt
convenient: it's not convenient	ça ne m'arrange pas	nuh ma-rahñzh pa
to cook (be cooking)	cuisiner	kwee-zee-nay
to cook a meal	préparer un repas	pray-pa-ray uñ ruh-pa
cooker	la cuisinière	kwee-zee-nyehr
to copy	copier	ko-pyay
corner	le coin	kwañ
corridor	le couloir	koo-lwar
cosmetics	les produits de beauté	pro-dwee duh boh-tay
cost	le coût	koo
to cost	coûter	koo-tay
how much does it cost?	ça coûte combien?	sa koot koñ-byañ

costume (swimming)	le maillot (de bain)	ma-yoh (duh bañ)
cough	la toux	too
cough mixture	le sirop pour la toux	see-roh poor la too
counter (shop, etc.)	le comptoir	koñ-twar
country (not town)	la campagne	kahñ-pa-nyuh
country (nation)	le pays	pay-ee
couple (two people)	le couple	koop-luh
a couple of...	deux...	duh...
course (syllabus)	le cours	koor
course (of meal)	le plat	pla
cover charge (restaurant)	le couvert	koo-vehr
crash (car)	l'accident m; la collision	lak-see-dahñ; ko-lee-zyoñ
cream (food, lotion)	la crème	krem
credit (on mobile phone)	les unités (fpl)	ew-nee-tay
credit card	la carte de crédit	kart duh kray-dee

crisps	les chips	sheep
to cross	traverser	tra-vehr-say
crossing (by sea)	la traversée	tra-vehr-say
crossroads	le carrefour; le croisement	kar-foor; krwaz-mahñ
cup	la tasse	tas
customer	le/la client(e)	klee-ahñ(t)
customs	la douane	dwan
(duty)	les droits de douane	drwa duh dwan
to cut	couper	koo-pay
to cycle	faire du vélo	fehr dew vay-loh

D

dairy produce	les produits laitiers	pro-dwee leh-tyay
dangerous	dangereux (-euse)	dahñ-zhuh-ruh(z)
date	la date	dat
date of birth	la date de naissance	dat duh neh-sahñs

English – French

daughter	la fille	fee
day	le jour	zhoor
per day	par jour	par zhoor
every day	tous les jours	too lay zhoor
deaf	sourd(d)	soor(d)
dear (expensive, in letter)	cher (chère)	shehr
debit card	la carte de paiement	kart duh pay-mahñ
decaffeinated coffee	décaféiné; le déca	ka-fay-ee-nay; day-ka
December	décembre	day-sahñbr
to declare	déclarer	day-kla-ray
nothing to declare	rien à déclarer	ryañ na day-kla-ray
delayed	retardé(e)	ruh-tar-day
delicatessen	l'épicerie fine f	ay-pees-ree feen
delicious	délicieux(-euse)	day-lee-syuh(z)
deodorant	le déodorant	day-oh-doh-rahñ
to depart	partir	par-teer

department store	le grand magasin	grahñ ma-ga-zañ
departure	le départ	day-par
departure lounge	la salle d'embarquement	sal dahñ-bar-kuh-mahñ
desk (furniture)	le bureau	bew-roh
desk (information)	l'accueil m	a-key
dessert	le dessert	deh-sehr
to develop (photos)	faire développer	fehr day-vloh-pay
diabetic	diabétique	dee-a-bay-teek
I'm diabetic	je suis diabétique	zhuh swee dee-a-bay-teek
to dial (a number)	composer	koñ-poh-say
dialling code	l'indicatif m	añ-dee-ka-teef
diesel	le diesel; le gasoil	dee-ay-zel; ga-zwal
diet	le régime	ray-zheem
I'm on a diet	je suis au régime	zhuh swee zoh ray-zheem
different	différent(e)	dee-fay-rahñ(t)

English	French	
difficult	difficile	dee-fee-seel
dining room	la salle à manger	sal a mahñ-zhay
dinner (evening meal)	le dîner	dee-nay
to have dinner	dîner	dee-nay
direct (train, etc.)	direct(e)	dee-rekt
directions	les indications	añ-dee-ka-syoñ
to ask for directions	demander le chemin	duh-mahñ-day luh shuh-mañ
dirty	sale	sal
disabled (person)	handicapé(e)	ahñ-dee-ka-pay
discount	le rabais	ra-beh
to disturb	déranger	day-rahñ-zhay
to dive	plonger	ploñ-zhay
divorced	divorcé(e)	dee-vor-say
dizzy	pris(e) de vertige	pree(z) duh vehr-teezh
to do	faire	fehr
doctor	le médecin	may-dsañ
documents	les papiers	pa-pyay
dollar	le dollar	do-lar

door	la porte	port
double bed	le grand lit	grahñ lee
double room	la chambre pour deux personnes	shahñbr poor duh pehr-son
down:		
to go down	descendre	deh-sahñdr
downstairs	en bas	ahñ ba
dress	la robe	rob
drink	la boisson	bwa-soñ
to drink	boire	bwar
drinking water	l'eau potable f	oh po-tabl
to drive	conduire	koñ-dweer
driver (of car)	le conducteur; la conductrice	koñ-dewk-tur; koñ-dewk-trees
driving licence	le permis de conduire	pehr-mee duh koñ-dweer
dry	sec (sèche)	sek/sesh
to dry	sécher	say-shay
dry-cleaner's	le pressing	preh-seeng
during	pendant	pahñ-dahñ
duty-free	hors taxe	or tax

English – French

English - French

E

each	chacun/ chacune	sha-kuñ/ sha-kewn
earlier	plus tôt	plew-toh
early	tôt	toh
east	l'est *m*	lest
Easter	Pâques	pak
easy	facile	fa-seel
to eat	manger	mahñ-zhay
either ... or	soit ... soit	swa ... swa
Elastoplast®	le sparadrap	spa-ra-dra
electric	électrique	ay-lek-treek
electricity	l'électricité *f*	ay-lek-tree-see-tay
electronic	électronique	ay-lek-tro-neek
elevator	l'ascenseur *m*	a-sahñ-sur
e-mail	l'e-mail *m*	ee-mehl
to e-mail	envoyer un e-mail	ahñ-vwa-yay uñ nee-mehl
e-mail address (on forms)	l'adresse électronique; le mél	a-dres ay-lek-tro-neek; mayl

embassy	l'ambassade *f*	ahñ-ba-sad
emergency	l'urgence *f*	ewr-zhahñs
emergency exit	la sortie de secours	sor-tee duh skoor
end	la fin	fañ
engaged (to be married)	fiancé(e)	fee-ahñ-say
engine	le moteur	moh-tur
England	l'Angleterre *f*	ahñ-gluh-tehr
English (language)	anglais(e)	ahñ-gleh(z)
to enjoy	aimer	ay-may
I enjoyed the trip	le voyage m'a plu	vwa-yazh ma plew
enough	assez	a-say
that's enough	ça suffit	sa sew-fee
enquiry desk	les renseignements	rahñ-seh-nyuh-mahñ
to enter	entrer	ahñ-tray
entrance	l'entrée *f*	ahñ-tray

English	French	Pronunciation
entrance fee	le prix d'entrée	pree dahñ-tray
equal	égal	ay-gal
error	l'erreur f	eh-rur
essential	indispensable	añ-dee-spahñ-sabl
euro (unit of currency)	l'euro m	uh-roh
European	l'Europe f	ur-op
European	européen(ne)	ur-o-pay-añ/en
evening	le soir	swar
this evening	ce soir	suh swar
in the evening	le soir	swar
every	chaque	shak
everyone	tout le monde	too luh moñd
everything	tout	too
everywhere	partout	pa-rtoo
example:		
for example	par exemple	par eg-zahñpl
excellent	excellent(e)	ek-seh-lahñ(t)
exchange	l'échange m	ay-shahñzh
exchange rate	le taux de change	toh duh shahñzh
to exchange	échanger	ay-shahñ-zhay
to excuse:		
excuse me! (to get by)	excusez-moi!	ek-skew-zay-mwa!
	pardon!	par-doñ!
exhibition	l'exposition f	ek-spoh-zee-syoñ
exit	la sortie	sor-tee
expensive	cher (chère)	shehr
to expire (ticket, passport, etc.)	expirer	ek-spee-ray
to explain	expliquer	ek-splee-kay
extra (additional)	supplémentaire	sew-play-mahñ-tehr
(more)	de plus	duh plews
eye	l'œil m	uhy
eyes	les yeux	yuh

F

English	French	Pronunciation
face	le visage	vee-zazh
facilities	les installations	añ-sta-la-syoñ

- to fall | tomber | toñ-bay
- he has fallen | il est tombé | eel eh toñ-bay
- family | la famille | fa-mee
- far | loin | lwañ
- is it far? | c'est loin? | say lwañ?
- fare (bus, etc.) | le prix du billet | pree dew bee-yeh
- farm | la ferme | fehrm
- fast | rapide | ra-peed
- too fast | trop vite | troh veet
- father | le père | pehr
- fault (defect) | un défaut | uñ day-foh
- it's not my fault | ce n'est pas de ma faute | suh nay pa duh ma foht
- fax | le fax | fax
- by fax | par fax | par fax
- fax number | le numéro de fax | new-may-roh duh fax
- to fax (document) | faxer | fak-say
- (person) | envoyer un fax à | añ-vwa-vay uñ fax a
- February | février | fay-vryay

- to feel | sentir | sahñ-teer
- I feel sick | j'ai la nausée | zhay la noh-say
- I don't feel well | je ne me sens pas bien | zhuh nuh muh sahñ pa byañ
- feet | les pieds | lay pyay
- fever | la fièvre | fyevr
- few | peu de | puh duh
- a few | quelques-un(e)s | kel-kuh-zuñ/zewn
- fiancé | le fiancé; | fee-yahñ-say
- fiancée | la fiancée |
- to fill in (form) | remplir | rahñ-pleer
- film (movie) | le film | feelm
- (for camera) | la pellicule | peh-lee-kewl
- to find | trouver | troo-vay
- fine (penalty) | la contravention | koñ-tra-vahñ-syoñ
- finger | le doigt | dwa
- to finish | finir | fee-neer
- finished | fini(e) | fee-nee
- fire | le feu; | fuh;
  | l'incendie m | añ-sahñ-dee

fire alarm	l'alarme d'incendie f	a-larm dañ-sahñ-dee
fire escape (staircase)	l'échelle de secours f	ay-shel duh skoor
first	premier(-ière)	pruh-myay/myehr
first aid	les premiers secours	pruh-myay skoor
first-class	de première classe	duh pruh-myehr klas
first name	le prénom	pray-noñ
fish	le poisson	pwa-soñ
fishing	la pêche	pesh
to go fishing	aller à la pêche	a-lay a la pesh
fit (medical)	l'attaque f	a-tak
to fit:		
it doesn't fit me	ça ne me va pas	sa nuh muh va pa
to fix (repair)	réparer	ray-pa-ray
can you fix it?	vous pouvez le réparer?	voo poo-vay luh ray-pa-ray?
flash (for camera)	le flash	flash
flat (apartment)	l'appartement m	a-par-tuh-mahñ

flavour (of ice cream, etc.)	le goût	goo
flight	le parfum	par-fuñ
floor (of room)	le vol	vol
(on the)	le sol	sol
ground floor (storey)	l'étage	ay-tazh
(on the) first	(au) rez-de-chaussée	(oh) ray-duh-shoh-say
floor	(au) premier étage	(oh) pruh-myayr ay-tazh
flour	la farine	fa-reen
flower	la fleur	flur
flu	la grippe	greep
to fly (bird)	aller en avion	a-lay ahñ na-vyoñ
	voler	vo-lay
food	la nourriture	noo-ree-tewr
food poisoning	l'intoxication alimentaire f	añ-tok-see-ka-syoñ a-lee-mahñ-tehr
foot	le pied	pyay
to go on foot	aller à pied	a-lay a pyay
for	pour	poor

English – French

English – French

English – French

(forbidden – go)

English – French

English	French	Pronunciation
for me/you/us	pour moi/vous/nous	poor mwa/voo/noo
for him/her/them	pour lui/elle/eux	poor lwee/el/uh
forbidden	interdit(e)	añ-tehr-dee(t)
foreign	étranger(-ère)	ay-trahñ-zhay/zhehr
fork (for eating)	la fourchette	foor-shet
form (document)	le formulaire	for-mew-lehr
form (shape, style)	la forme	form
fortnight	la quinzaine	kañ-zen
fountain	la fontaine	foñ-ten
fragile	fragile	fra-zheel
France	la France	frahñs
in/to France	en France	ahñ frahñs
free (not occupied)	libre	leebr
free (costing nothing)	gratuit(e)	gra-twee(t)
freezer	le congélateur	koñ-zhayla-tur
French (language)	le français	frahñ-seh(z)
French fries	les frites	frahñ-seh / freet
fresh	frais (fraîche)	freh/fresh
Friday	vendredi	vahñ-druh-dee
fried	frit(e)	free(t)
friend m/f	l'ami(e)	a-mee
from	de	duh
I'm from England	je suis anglais(e)	zhuh swee zahñ-gleh(z)
I'm from Scotland	je suis écossais(e)	zhuh swee zay-ko-seh(z)
front	le devant	duh-vahñ
in front of...	devant...	duh-vahñ...
frozen	gelé(e)	zhuh-lay
fruit	le fruit	frwee
fruit juice	le jus de fruit	jew duh frwee
full (container)	plein(e)	plañ/plen
full board (e.g. hall)	complet(-ète)	koñ-pleh(t)
furnished	la pension complète	pahñ-syoñ koñ-plet
	meublé(e)	muh-blay

G

gallery	la galerie	gal-ree
game	le jeu	zhuh
garage	la station-service	sta-syoñ-sehr-vees
(for petrol)		
(for parking, repair)	le garage	ga-razh
garden	le jardin	zhar-dañ
garlic	l'ail m	a-yuh
gate	la porte	port
gents' (toilet)	les toilettes pour hommes	twa-let poor om
German (language)	allemand(e)	al-mahñ(d)
German m		al-mahñ
Germany f	l'Allemagne f	a-luh-ma-nyuh
to get (obtain)	obtenir	ob-tuh-neer
(to fetch)	aller chercher	a-lay shehr-shay
to get in (vehicle)	monter	moñ-tay
to get off	descendre	deh-sahñdr
(bus, etc.)		
gift	le cadeau	ka-doh

gift shop	la boutique de souvenirs	boo-teek duh soo-vneer
girl	la fille	fee
girlfriend	la copine	ko-peen
to give	donner	do-nay
to give back	rendre	rahñdr
glass	le verre	vehr
a glass of water	un verre d'eau	uñ vehr doh
glasses	les lunettes	lew-net
(spectacles)		
gluten	le gluten	glew-ten
to go	aller	a-lay
I'm going to...	je vais à...	zhuh veh a...
(I will go to)		
I'm going to...	je vais...	zhuh veh...
(I intend to)		
we're going to hire a car	nous allons louer une voiture	noo za-loñ loo-ay ewn vwa-tewr
to go back	retourner	ruh-toor-nay
to go in	entrer	ahñ-tray

English - French

English – French

to go out (leave)	sortir	sor-teer
good	bon (bonne)	boñ (bon)
(that's) good!	(c'est) bien!	(say) byañ!
good afternoon	bonjour	boñ-zhoor
goodbye	au revoir	oh ruh-vwar
good night	bonne nuit	bon nwee
grandchildren	les petits-enfants	puh-tee zahñ-fañ
grandparents	les grands-parents	grahñ-pa-rahñ
grape	le raisin	reh-zañ
great (big)	grand(e)	grahñ(d)
great (wonderful)	formidable	for-mee-dabl
Great Britain	la Grande-Bretagne	grahñd-bruh-ta-nyuh
green	vert(e)	vehr(t)
greengrocer's	le magasin de fruits et légumes	ma-ga-zañ duh fwee zay lay-gewm
grilled	grillé(e)	gree-yay
grocer's	l'épicerie f	ay-pee-sree

ground floor	le rez-de-chaussée	ray-duh-shoh-say
on the ground floor	au rez-de-chaussée	oh ray-duh-shoh-say
group	le groupe	group
guest (in house)	l'invité(e)	añ-vee-tay
guest (in hotel)	le/la client(e)	klee-ahñ(t)
guesthouse	la pension	pahñ-syoñ
guide (tourist)	le/la guide	geed
guidebook	le guide	geed
guided tour	la visite guidée	vee-zeet gee-day

H

hair	les cheveux	shuh-vuh
hairdryer	le sèche-cheveux	sesh-shuh-vuh
half	la moitié	mwa-tyay
half an hour	une demi-heure	ewn duh-mee-ur
half board	la demi-pension	duh-mee-pahñ-syoñ
ham (cooked)	le jambon	zhahñ-boñ
ham (cured)	le jambon cru	zhahñ-boñ krew

hamburger	le hamburger	ahñ-bur-ger
hand	la main	mañ
handbag	le sac à main	sak a mañ
handicapped	handicapé(e)	ahñ-dee-ka-pay
to happen	arriver; se passer	suh pa-say
what happened?	qu'est-ce qui s'est passé?	kes kee say pa-say?
happy	heureux(-euse)	uh-ruh(z)
hard (not soft)	dur(e)	dewr
(not easy)	difficile	dee-fee-seel
to have	avoir	av-war
to have to	devoir	duh-war
hay fever	le rhume des foins	rewm day fwañ
he	il	eel
head	la tête	tet
headache	le mal de tête	mal duh tet
I have a headache	j'ai mal à la tête	zhay mal a la tet
health	la santé	sahñ-tay
to hear	entendre	ahñ-tahñdr

heart	le cœur	kur
heartburn	les brûlures d'estomac	brew-lewr d'es-toh-ma
heating	le chauffage	shoh-fazh
heavy	lourd(e)	loor(d)
hello	bonjour	boñ-zhoor
(on telephone)	allô?	a-loh?
help!	au secours!	oh skoor!
can you help me?	vous pouvez m'aider?	voo poo-vay meh-day?
her	son/sa/ses	soñ/sa/say
her passport	son passeport	soñ pas-por
her suitcases	ses valises	say va-leez
herbal tea	la tisane	tee-zan
here	ici	ee-see
here is...	voici...	vwa-see...
hi!	salut!	sa-lew!
high	haut(e)	oh(t)
him	lui	lwee
to hire	louer	loo-ay

English – French

English	French	Pronunciation
hired car	la voiture de location	la wa-tewr duh lo-ka-syoñ
his	son/sa/ses	soñ/sa/say
his passport	son passeport	soñ pas-por
his suitcases	ses valises	say va-leez
on holiday	en vacances	añ va-kañs
home	la maison	la may-zoñ
at my/your/ our home	chez moi/vous/ nous	shay mwa/voo/ noo
honey	le miel	myel
I hope so/not	j'espère que oui/non	zheh-spehr kuh wee/noñ
hospital	l'hôpital m	o-pee-tal
hostel (youth hostel)	l'auberge de jeunesse f	oh-behzh duh zhuh-nes
hot	chaud(e)	shoh(d)
I'm hot	j'ai chaud	zhay shoh
it's hot (weather)	il fait chaud	eel feh shoh
hotel	l'hôtel m	oh-tel
hour	l'heure f	ur

English (italic)	French	Pronunciation
half an hour	une demi-heure	ewn duh-mee ur
house	la maison	meh-soñ
house wine	le vin en pichet	vañ añ pee-sheh
how	comment	ko-mañ
how much/ many?	combien?	koñ-byañ?
how are you?	comment allez-vous?	ko-mañ ta-lay voo?
hungry:		
to be hungry	avoir faim	awar fañ
I'm hungry	j'ai faim	zhay fañ
hurry:		
I'm in a hurry	je suis pressé(e)	zhuh swee preh-say
to hurt	faire du mal	fehr dew mal
to hurt somebody	à quelqu'un	a kel-kuñ
that hurts	ça fait mal	sa feh mal
husband	le mari	ma-ree

I	je	zhuh
ice	la glace	glas
(cube)	le glaçon	gla-soñ
with/without ice	avec/sans glaçons	a-vek/sañ gla-soñ
ice cream	la glace	glas
identity card	la carte d'identité	kart dee-dahñ-tee-tay
if	si	see
ill	malade	ma-lad
illness	la maladie	ma-la-dee
important	important(e)	añ-por-tahñ(t)
impossible	impossible	añ-po-seebl
in	dans	dahñ
in two hours' time	dans deux heures	dahñ duh zur
in front of	devant	duh-vahñ
included	compris(e)	koñ-pree(z)
indigestion	l'indigestion f	añ-dee-zhes-tyoñ
information	les renseignements	rahñ-seh-nyuh-mahñ
injured	blessé(e)	bleh-say
inside	à l'intérieur	a lañ-tay-ryur
instead of	au lieu de	oh lyuh duh
insurance	l'assurance f	a-sew-rahñs
insurance certificate	l'attestation d'assurance f	a-tes-ta-syoñ da-sew-rahñs
insured	assuré(e)	a-sew-ray
interesting	intéressant(e)	añ-tay-reh-sahñ(t)
international	international(e)	añ-tehr-na-syo-nal
into	dans; en	dahñ; ahñ
into town	en ville	ahñ veel
Ireland	l'Irlande f	eer-lahñd
Irish	irlandaise(e)	eer-lahñ-deh(z)
iron (for clothes)	le fer à repasser	fehr a ruh-pa-say
is	est	ay
island	l'île f	leel

English – French

English – French

it	il/elle	eel/el
Italian	italien(ne)	ee-ta-lyañ/yen
Italy	l'Italie f	ee-ta-lee
to itch	démanger	day-mañ-zhay
it itches	*ça me démange*	*sa muh day-mahñzh*

J

January	janvier	jahñ-vyay
jeweller's	la bijouterie	bee-zhoo-tree
jewellery	les bijoux	bee-zhoo
job	le travail; l'emploi	tra-va-yuh; ahñ-plwa
journey	le voyage	vwa-yazh
juice	le jus	jew
fruit juice	*le jus de fruit*	*jew duh fwee*
orange juice	*le jus d'orange*	*jew do-rahñzh*
July	juillet	zhwee-yeh
June	juin	zhwañ

K

to keep (retain)	garder	gar-day
keep the change	*gardez la monnaie*	*gar-day la mo-neh*
key	la clé/clef	klay
car key	*la clé/clef de la voiture*	*klay duh vwa-tewr*
kilo(gram)	le kilo	kee-loh
kilometre	le kilomètre	kee-loh-metr
kiosk (newstand) (phone box)	le kiosque	kee-yosk
kitchen	la cabine la cuisine	ka-been kwee-zeen
knee	le genou	zhuh-noo
knife	le couteau	koo-toh
to know (how to do, to be aware of)	savoir	sa-vwar
	connaître	ko-nehtr
I don't know	*je ne sais pas*	*zhuh nuh seh pa*
I don't know Paris	*je ne connais pas Paris*	*zhuh nuh ko-neh pa pa-ree*

L

ladies' (toilet)	les toilettes pour dames	twa-let poor dam
lamb	l'agneau *m*	a-nyoh
to land	atterrir	a-teh-reer
language	la langue	lahñg
large	grand(e)	grahñ(d)
last	dernier(-ière)	dehr-nyay/nyehr
last month	le mois dernier	mwa dehr-nyay
last night (evening)	hier soir	ee-yehr swar
(night-time)	la nuit dernière	nwee dehr-nyehr
last week	la semaine dernière	suh-men dehr-nyehr
late	tard	tar
later	plus tard	plew tar
lavatory	les toilettes	twa-let
to leave (depart for)	partir	par-teer
(depart from)	quitter	kee-tay
(to leave behind)	laisser	leh-say
to leave for *Paris*	partir pour Paris	par-teer poor pa-ree
to leave *London*	quitter Londres	kee-tay loñdr
left:		
on/to the left	à gauche	a gohsh
left-luggage (office)	la consigne	koñ-see-nyuh
leg	la jambe	zhahñb
lemon	le citron	see-troñ
lemonade	la limonade	lee-mo-nad
lens (contact lens)	la lentille	lahñ-tee
less	moins	mo-añ
less than	moins de	mwañ duh
letter	la lettre	letr
lift (elevator)	l'ascenseur *m*	a-sahñ-sur
light (not heavy)	léger(-ère)	lay-zhay/zhehr
light	la lumière	lewm-yehr
have you got a light?	avez-vous du feu?	a-vay-voo dew fuh?
like (preposition)	comme	kom

English – French

English – French

English	French	Pronunciation
like this	comme ça	kom sa
to like	aimer	eh-may
I like coffee	j'aime le café	zhem luh ka-fay
I don't like coffee	je n'aime pas le café	zhuh nem pa luh ka-fay
I'd like...	je voudrais...	zhuh voo-dreh...
we'd like...	nous voudrions...	noo voo-dryoñ...
line (queue)	la file	feel
(telephone)	la ligne	lee-nyuh
to listen to	écouter	ay-koo-tay
litre	le litre	leetr
little	petit(e)	puh-tee(t)
a little...	un peu de...	uñ puh duh...
to live (in a place)	vivre; habiter	veevr; a-bee-tay
I live in London	j'habite à Londres	zha-beet a lañdr
to lock	fermer à clé/clef	fe-rmay a klay
London	Londres	lañdr
to/in London	à Londres	a lañdr
long	long(ue)	loñ(g)
for a long time	longtemps	loñ-tañ
to look after	garder	gar-day
to look at	regarder	ruh-gar-day
to look for	chercher	shehr-shay
to lose	perdre	pehrdr
lost (object)	perdu(e)	pehr-dew
I've lost...	j'ai perdu...	zhay pehr-dew...
I'm lost	je suis perdu(e)	zhuh swee pehr-dew
lost property office	le bureau des objets trouvés	bew-roh day zob-zheh troo-vay
lot: a lot of	beaucoup de	boh-koo duh
loud	fort(e)	for(t)
lounge (in hotel, airport)	le salon	sa-loñ
love	l'amour	a-moor
to love (person)	aimer	eh-may
I love you	je t'aime	zhuh tem
I love (food, activity, etc.)	adorer	a-do-ray
I love swimming	j'adore nager	zha-dor na-zhay
lovely	beau (belle)	boh (bel)

English	French	Pronunciation
low	bas (basse)	ba(s)
luck	la chance	shahñs
lucky	chanceux(euse)	shahñ-suh(z)
luggage	les bagages	ba-gazh
luggage trolley	le chariot	sha-ryoh
lunch	le déjeuner	day-zhuh-nay
luxury	le luxe	lewx
M		
machine	la machine	ma-sheen
magazine	la revue; le magazine	ruh-vew; ma-ga-zeen
mail	le courrier	koo-ryay
by mail	par la poste	par la post
main	principal(e)	prañ-see-pal
to make	faire	fehr
make-up	le maquillage	ma-kee-yazh
male (person)	masculin	mas-kew-lañ
man	l'homme *m*	om
manager	le/la directeur (-trice)	dee-rek-tur (-rek-trees)
many	beaucoup de	boh-koo duh
map	la carte	kart
road map	la carte routière	kart roo-tyehr
street map	le plan de la ville	plahñ duh la veel
March	mars	mars
market	le marché	mar-shay
married	marié(e)	ma-ryay
I'm married	je suis marié(e)	zhuh swee ma-ray
mass (in church)	la messe	mes
match (sport)	le match	match
matches	les allumettes	alew-met
to matter: *it doesn't matter*	ça ne fait rien	sa nuh feh ryañ
what's the matter?	qu'est-ce qu'il y a?	kes keel ya?
May	mai	meh
me	moi	mwa
meal	le repas	ruh-pa
to mean	vouloir dire	voo-lwar deer
what does this mean?	qu'est-ce que ça veut dire?	kes kuh sa vuh deer?

English	French	Pronunciation
meat	la viande	wahñd
medicine	le médicament	may-dee-ka-mahñ
Mediterranean Sea	la Méditerranée	may-dee-tay-ra-nay
to meet	rencontrer	rahñ-koñ-tray
meeting	la réunion	ray-ew-nyoñ
men	les hommes	om
to mend	réparer	ray-pa-ray
menu (set meal)	le menu	muh-new
(card)	la carte	kart
message	le message	meh-sazh
meter	le compteur	koñ-tur
metre	le mètre	metr
metro	le métro	may-troh
metro station	la station de métro	sta-syoñ duh may-troh
midday	midi	mee-dee
at midday	à midi	a mee-dee
middle	le milieu	mee-lyuh
midnight	minuit	mee-nwee
at midnight	à minuit	a mee-nwee
mild (weather, cheese)	doux (douce)	doo(s)
(curry)	peu épicé(e)	puh ay-pee-say
(tobacco)	léger(ère)	lay-zhay/zhehr
milk	le lait	leh
baby milk (formula)	le lait maternisé	leh ma-tehr-nee-zay
fresh milk	le lait frais	leh freh
soya milk	le lait de soja	leh duh so-zha
with/without milk	avec/sans lait	a-vek/sahñ leh
to mind: do you mind if I...?	ça vous gêne si je...?	sa voo zhen see zhuh...?
I don't mind do you mind?	ça m'est égal vous permettez?	sa may tay-gal voo pehr-meh-tay?
mineral water	l'eau minérale f	oh mee-nay-ral
minute	la minute	la mee-newt
to miss (train, flight, etc.)	rater	ra-tay
Miss	Mademoiselle	ma-dmwa-zel

English	French	Pronunciation
missing (disappeared)	disparu(e)	dee-spa-rew
mistake	l'erreur *f*	eh-rur
mobile (phone)	le mobile; le portable	mo-beel; por-tabl
mobile number	le numéro de mobile/ portable	new-may-roh duh mo-beel/ por-tabl
moment: at the moment	en ce moment	añ suh mo-mañ
Monday	lundi	luñ-dee
money	l'argent *m*	ar-zhañ
I have no money	je n'ai pas d'argent	zhuh nay pa dar-zhañ
month	le mois	mwa
this month	ce mois-ci	suh mwa-see
next month	le mois prochain	mwa pro-shañ
more	encore	añ-kor
more wine	plus de vin	plews duh vañ
more than	plus de	plews duh
morning	le matin	ma-tañ
in the morning	le matin	luh ma-tañ
tomorrow morning	demain matin	duh-mañ ma-tañ
mother	la mère	mehr
motorbike	la moto	moh-toh
motorway	l'autoroute *f*	oh-toh-root
mountain	la montagne	moñ-ta-nyuh
mouth	la bouche	boosh
to move	bouger	boo-zhay
movie	le film	feelm
Mr	Monsieur	muh-syuh
Mrs	Madame	ma-dam
Ms	Madame	ma-dam
much: *too much*	trop	troh
museum	le musée	mew-zay
music	la musique	mew-zeek
must	devoir	duh-vwar
my	mon/ma/mes	moñ/ma/may

N

English	French	Pronunciation
name	le nom	luh noñ

English – French

English	French	Pronunciation
my name is...	je m'appelle...	zhuh ma-pel...
what is your name?	comment vous appelez-vous?	ko-mahñ voo za-play voo?
nationality	la nationalité	na-syo-na-lee-tay
near	près de	preh duh
is it near?	c'est près d'ici?	say preh dee-see?
to need (to)	avoir besoin de	a-war buh-zwañ duh
I need...	j'ai besoin	zhay buh-zwañ
new	nouveau(-elle)	noo-vo/vel
news (TV, etc.)	les informations	añ-for-ma-syoñ
newspaper	le journal	zhoor-nal
New Zealand	la Nouvelle-Zélande	noo-vel zay-lahñd
next (after)	prochain(e)	pro-shañ
	ensuite	ahñ-sweet
next Monday	lundi prochain	luñ-dee pro-shañ
the next train	le prochain train	pro-shañ trañ
next week	la semaine prochaine	suh-men pro-shen
next to	à côté de	a ko-tay duh

English	French	Pronunciation
nice (enjoyable)	beau (belle)	boh (bel)
(person)	bon (bonne)	boñ (bon)
	sympathique	sañ-pa-teek
night (night-time)	la nuit	nwee
(evening)	le soir	swar
last night	hier soir	ee-yehr swar
tomorrow night (evening)	demain soir	duh-mañ swar
tonight	ce soir	suh swar
nightclub	la boîte de nuit	bwat duh nwee
no	non	noñ
(without)	sans	sahñ
no thanks	non merci	noñ mehr-see
noisy: it's very noisy	il y a beaucoup de bruit	eel ya boh-koo de brwee
non-smoking (seat, compartment)	non fumeurs	noñ few-mur
north	le nord	nor
Northern Ireland	l'Irlande du Nord f	eer-lahñd dew nor
nose	le nez	nay

English	French	Pronunciation
not	ne ... pas	nuh ... pa
I am not...	je ne suis pas...	zhuh nuh swee pa...
note (banknote)	le billet	bee-yeh
nothing	rien	ryañ
November	novembre	no-vahñbr
now	maintenant	mañ-tuh-nahñ
number (quantity)	le nombre	noñbr
(of room, house)	le numéro	new-may-roh
phone number	le numéro de téléphone	new-may-roh duh tay-lay-fon

O

October	octobre	ok-tobr
of	de	duh
a glass of...	un verre de...	uñ vehr duh...
made of...	en...	ahñ...
office	le bureau	bew-roh
often	souvent	soo-vahñ
oil (for car, food)	l'huile *f*	weel
OK (agreed)	d'accord	da-kor

(good)	bon (bonne)	boñ (bon)
old	vieux (vieille)	vyuh (vyeh-yuh)
how old are you?	quel âge avez-vous?	kel azh a-vay voo?
I'm ... years old	j'ai ... ans	zhay ... ahñ
on (light)	allumé(e)	a-lew-may
(machine, etc)	en marche	ahñ marsh
on the table	sur la table	sewr la tabl
on time	à l'heure	a lur
once	une fois	ewn fwa
onion	l'oignon *m*	loh-nyoñ
open	ouvert(e)	oo-vehr
opposite	en face de	ahñ fas duh
or	ou	oo
orange (fruit)	l'orange	o-rahñzh
(colour)	orange	o-rahñzh
orange juice	le jus d'orange	jew do-rahñzh
order: out of order	en panne	ahñ pan
to order	commander	ko-mahñ-day
other	autre	ohtr

English	French	pronunciation
have you any others?	vous en avez d'autres?	voo zahñ na·vay dohtr?
our (singular)	notre	notr
our (plural)	nos	noh
our room	notre chambre	notr shahñbr
our baggage	nos bagages	noh ba·gazh
outside	dehors	duh·or
P		
to pack (luggage)	faire les bagages	fehr lay ba·gazh
package	le paquet	pa·kay
page	la page	pazh
paid	payé(e)	pay·yay
I've paid	j'ai payé	zhay pay·yay
pain	la douleur	doo·lur
painful	douloureux (-euse)	doo·loo·ruh(z)
painkiller	l'analgésique *m*	a·nal·zhay·zeek
pants (underwear)	le slip;	sleep;
(trousers)	le pantalon	pahñ·ta·loñ
paper	le papier	pa·pyay

pardon?	comment?	ko·mahñ?
parents	les parents	pa·rahñ
park	le parc	park
to park	garer (la voiture)	ga·ray(la wa·tewr)
party (group)	le groupe	groop
(celebration)	la fête; la soirée	fet; swa·ray
pass (bus, train)	la carte	kart
passenger	le passager;	pa·sa·zhay;
	la passagère	pa·sa·zhehr
passport	le passeport	pas·por
pasta	les pâtes	pat
pastry	la pâte	pat
(cake)	la pâtisserie	pa·tee·sree
to pay	payer	pay·yay
I'd like to pay	je voudrais payer	zhuh voo·dreh pay·yay
where do I pay?	où est-ce qu'il faut payer?	oo es keel foh pay·yay?
peanut	la cacahuète	ka·ka·wet
peanut allergy	l'allergie aux cacahuètes	a·lehr·zhee oh ka·ka·wet

English	French	Pronunciation
peas	les petits pois	puh-tee pwa
pen	le stylo	stee-loh
pensioner	le/la retraité(e)	ruh-treh-tay
people	les gens	zhahñ
pepper (spice)	le poivre	pwavr
pepper (vegetable)	le poivron	pwa-vroñ
per: per day	par jour	par zhoor
per hour	à l'heure	a lur
per person	par personne	par pehr-son
per week	par semaine	par suh-men
performance	le spectacle	spek-takl
person	la personne	pehr-son
petrol	l'essence f	eh-sahñs
unleaded	l'essence sans plomb	eh-sahñs sahñ ploñ
petrol station	la station-service	sta-syoñ ser-vees
pharmacy	la pharmacie	far-ma-see
to photocopy	photocopier	foh-toh-ko-pyay
photograph	la photo	foh-toh

English	French	Pronunciation
to take a photograph	prendre une photo	prahñdr ewn foh-toh
piece	le morceau	mor-soh
pink	rose	roz
place of birth	le lieu de naissance	lyuh duh neh-sahñs
plan (map)	le plan	plahñ
plate	l'assiette f	a-syet
platform (railway)	le quai	keh
which platform?	quel quai?	kel keh?
play (at theatre)	la pièce	pyes
please	s'il vous plaît	seel voo pleh
pleased to meet you	enchanté(e)	ahñ-shahñ-tay
poisonous	vénéneux	vay-nay-nuh
police (force)	la police	po-lees
police station	le commissariat; la gendarmerie	ko-mee-sa-rya; zhahñ-dar-mree
pork	le porc	por
port (seaport)	le port	por
porter (for luggage)	le porteur	por-tur

English – French

202 | 203

English	French	Pronunciation
possible	possible	po-seebl
post (letters)	le courrier	koo-ryay
by post	par courrier	par koo-ryay
to post	poster	po-stay
postbox	la boîte aux lettres	bwat oh letr
postcard	la carte postale	kart po-stal
post office	la poste	post
potato	la pomme de terre	pom duh tehr
pound (weight, money)	la livre	leevr
to prefer	préférer	pray-fa-yray
pregnant	enceinte	ahñ-sañt
present (gift)	le cadeau	ka-doh
pretty	joli(e)	zho-lee
price	le prix	pree
price list	le tarif	ta-reef
problem	le problème	pro-blem
prohibited	interdit(e)	añ-tehr-dee
public	public(-ique)	pew-bleek
pudding	le dessert	deh-sehr
to pull	tirer	tee-ray
purse	le porte-monnaie	port-mo-neh
to push	pousser	poo-say
Q		
quarter	le quart	kar
question	la question	ke-styoñ
quick	rapide	ra-peed
quickly	vite	veet
quiet (place)	tranquille	trahñ-keel
quite (rather)	assez	a-say
(completely)	complètement	koñ-plet-mahñ
quite good	pas mal	pa mal
R		
railway	le chemin de fer	shuh-mañ duh fehr
railway station	la gare	gar
to rain:		
it's raining	il pleut	eel pluh

English – French

English	French	Pronunciation
rare (steak)	saignant(e)	say-nyahñ(t)
rate of exchange	le taux de change	toh duh shahñzh
raw	cru(e)	crew
razor	le rasoir	ra-zwar
razor blades	les lames de rasoir	lam duh ra-zwar
ready	prêt(e)	preh/pret
receipt	le reçu	ruh-sew
reception (desk)	la réception	ray-sep-syoñ
to recommend	recommander	ruh-ko-mahñ-day
red	rouge	roozh
reduction	la réduction	ray-dewk-syoñ
remember	se rappeler	suh ra-play
I don't remember	je ne m'en rappelle pas	zhuh nuh mahñ ra-pel pa
to repair	réparer	ray-pa-ray
to repeat	répéter	ray-pay-tay
to report (theft, etc.)	déclarer	day-kla-ray
reservation	la réservation	ray-zehr-va-syoñ
to reserve	réserver	ray-zehr-vay
reserved	réservé(e)	ray-zehr-vay
rest (relaxation)	le repos	ruh-poh
rest (remainder)	le reste	rest
restaurant	le restaurant	reh-stoh-rahñ
retired	retraité(e)	ruh-treh-tay
to return (to a place)	retourner	ruh-toor-nay
return ticket	le billet aller-retour	bee-yeh a-lay-ruh-toor
rice	le riz	ree
right (correct)	exact(e)	eg-zakt
right (not left)	à droite	drwat
on/to the right	à droite	a drwat
river	la rivière	ree-vyehr
Riviera (French)	la Côte d'Azur	koht da-zewr
road	la route	root
road map	la carte rout ère	kart roo-tyehr
road sign	le panneau	pa-noh
roll (bread)	le petit pain	puh-tee pañ

room (in house)	la pièce	pyes
(in hotel)	la chambre	shahñbr
double room	la chambre pour deux personnes	shahñbr poor duh pehr-son
family room	la chambre pour une famille	shahñbr poor ewn fa-mee
single room	la chambre pour une personne	shahñbr poor ewn pehr-son
room number	le numéro de chambre	new-may-roh duh shahñbr
room service	le service des chambres	sehr-vees day shahñbr

S

safe (for valuables)	le coffre-fort	kofr-for
is it safe?	ce n'est pas dangereux?	suh nay pa dahñ-zhuh-ruh?
salad	la salade	sa-lad
salad dressing	la vinaigrette	vee-neh-gret
salesman/ woman	le vendeur; la vendeuse	vahñ-dur; vahñ-duhz

salt	le sel	sel
sandwich	le sandwich	sahñ-dweetsh
toasted sandwich	le croque-monsieur	krok-muh-syuh
Saturday	samedi	sam-dee
sauce	la sauce	sohs
sausage	la saucisse	so-sees
to say	dire	deer
scarf (silk)	le foulard	foo-lar
(woollen)	l'écharpe f	ay-sharp
school	l'école f	ay-kol
Scotland	l'Écosse f	ay-kos
Scottish	écossais(e)	ay-ko-say
scuba diving	la plongée sous-marine	ploñ-zhay soo-ma-reen
sea	la mer	mehr
seafood	les fruits de mer	frwee duh mehr
season (of year)	la saison	seh-zoñ
seat (chair)	le siège	syezh
(in train)	la place	plas
(cinema, theatre)	le fauteuil	foh-tuh-yuh

English	French	pronunciation
second	deuxième; second(e)	duh-zyem; suh-koñ(d)
second class	seconde classe	suh-koñd klas
to see	voir	vwar
to sell	vendre	vahñdr
do you sell...?	vous vendez...?	voo vahñ-day...?
to send	envoyer	ahñ-wa-yay
September	septembre	sep-tahñbr
service	le service	sehr-vees
is service included?	le service est compris?	sehr-vees ay koñ-pree?
shampoo	le shampooing	shahñ-pwañ
shaver	le rasoir électrique	ra-zwar ay-lek-treek
she	elle	el
sheet (for bed)	le drap	dra
shirt	la chemise	shuh-meez
shoe	la chaussure	shoh-sewr
shop	le magasin	ma-ga-zañ
to shop	faire du shopping	fehr dew sho-peeng

English	French	pronunciation
shop assistant	le vendeur; la vendeuse	vahñ-dur; vahñ-duhz
shopping centre	le centre commercial	sahñtr ko-mehr-syal
short	court(e)	koor(t)
le short		short
shoulder	l'épaule f	ay-pohl
show	le spectacle	spek-takl
shower (wash)	la douche	doosh
to have/take a shower	prendre une douche	prahñdr ewn doosh
shower gel	le gel douche	zhel doosh
sick (ill)	malade	ma-lad
I feel sick	j'ai envie de vomir	zhay ahñ-vee duh vo-meer
sign (notice)	le panneau	pa-noh
silk	la soie	swa
silver	l'argent m	ar-zhahñ
similar (to)	semblable (à)	sahñ-blabl(a)
since	depuis	duh-pwee

English – French

English – French

English	French	Pronunciation
single (unmarried) (bed, room)	célibataire pour une personne	say-lee-ba-tehr / poor ewn pehr-son
single ticket	l'aller simple m	a-lay sañpl
sir	Monsieur	muh-syuh
sister	la sœur	sur
size (clothes)	la taille	ta-yuh
size (shoe)	la pointure	pwañ-tewr
ski	le ski	skee
ski lift	le remonte-pente	ruh-moñt pañt
ski pass	le forfait	for-feh
to ski	faire du ski	fehr dew skee
skin	la peau	poh
skirt	la jupe	zhewp
to sleep	dormir	dor-meer
slice (bread, salami, etc.)	la tranche	trañsh
	la part	par
slow	lent(e)	lañ(t)
slowly	lentement	lañ-tuh-mañ
small	petit(e)	puh-tee(t)
to smoke	fumer	few-may
I don't smoke	je ne fume pas	zhuh nuh fewm pa
can I smoke?	on peut fumer?	oñ puh few-may?
smoked	fumé(e)	few-may
snack	le casse-croûte	kas-kroot
snail	l'escargot m	es-kar-goh
snow	la neige	nezh
soap	le savon	sa-voñ
socks	les chaussettes	shoh-set
soft drink	le soda	so-da
some	du/de la/des	dew/duh la/day
someone	quelqu'un	kel-kuñ
something	quelque chose	kel-kuh shohz
sometimes	quelquefois	kel-kuh fwa
son	le fils	fees
soon	bientôt	byañ-toh
as soon as possible	dès que possible	deh kuh / po-seebl
sore: to have a sore throat	avoir mal à la gorge	a-war mal a la gorzh

English	French	Pronunciation
sorry: I'm sorry	excusez-moi	ek-skew-say-mwa
soup	le potage; la soupe	po-tazh; soop
south	le sud	sewd
Spain	l'Espagne f	es-pa-nyuh
Spanish	espagnol(e)	es-pa-nyol
sparkling (wine)	mousseux(-euse)	moo-suh(z)
(water)	gazeux(-euse)	ga-zuh(z)
to speak	parler	par-lay
do you speak English?	vous parlez anglais?	voo par-lay ahñgleh?
speciality	la spécialité	spay-sya-lee-tay
speed limit	la limitation de vitesse	lee-mee-ta-syoñ duh vee-tes
to spend (money)	dépenser	day-pahñ-say
(time)	passer	pa-say
spoon	la cuiller	kwee-yehr
sport	le sport	spor
spring (season)	le printemps	prañ-tahñ
square (in town)	la place	plas
squid	le calmar	calmar
stamp	le timbre	tañbr
to start	commencer	ko-mahñ-say
station	la gare	gar
stay	le séjour	say-zhoor
enjoy your stay	bon séjour	boñ say-zhoor
to stay (remain)	rester	res-tay
(reside for while)	loger	lo-zhay
I'm staying at...	je loge à...	zhuh lozh a...
steak	le bifteck	beef-tek
sterling	la livre sterling	leevr stehr-leeng
still: still water	l'eau plate f	oh plat
stolen	volé(e)	vo-lay
stomach	l'estomac m	es-to-ma
to have a stomach ache	avoir mal au ventre	a-vwar mal oh vahñtr
to stop	arrêter	a-reh-tay
store (shop)	le magasin	ma-ga-zañ
storey	l'étage m	ay-tazh
straight on	tout droit	too drwa
strawberries	les fraises	frez
street	la rue	rew

English – French

English – French

street map	le plan des rues	plahñ day rew
strong	fort(e)	for(t)
student	l'étudiant(e)	ay-tew-dyahñ(t)
student discount	le tarif étudiant	ta-reef ay-tew-dyahñ
stung	piqué(e)	pee-kay
suede	le daim	dañ
sugar	le sucre	sewkr
sugar-free	sans sucre	sahñ sewkr
suit (man's)	le costume	kos-tewm
suitcase	la valise	va-leez
summer	l'été m	ay-tay
sun	le soleil	so-leh-yuh
to sunbathe	prendre un bain de soleil	prahñdr uñ bañ duh so-leh-yuh
sunburn	le coup de soleil	koo duh so-leh-yuh
suncream	la crème solaire	krem so-lehr
Sunday	le dimanche	dee-mahñsh

sunglasses	les lunettes de soleil	lew-net duh so-leh-yuh
sunny: it's sunny	il fait beau	eel feh boh
supermarket	le supermarché	sew-pehr-mar-shay
supper (dinner)	le souper	soo-pay
supplement	le supplément	sew-play-mahñ
surname	le nom de famille	noñ duh fa-mee
sweetener	l'édulcorant m	ay-dewl-ko-rahñ
sweets	les bonbons	boñ-boñ
to swim	nager	na-zhay
swimming pool	la piscine	pee-seen
swimsuit	le maillot de bain	ma-yoh duhbañ
Swiss	suisse	swees
to switch off	éteindre	ay-tañdr
to switch on	allumer	a-lew-may
Switzerland	la Suisse	swees
swollen	enflé(e)	ahñ-flay

T

table	la table	tabl

English	French	Pronunciation
table tennis	le tennis de table	teh-nees duh tabl
table wine	le vin de table	vañ duh tabl
tablet	le comprimé	koñ-pree-may
to take	prendre	prahñdr
to talk (to)	parler (à)	par-lay (a)
tall	grand(e)	grahñ(d)
tart	la tarte	tart
to taste	goûter	goo-tay
can I taste it	je peux goûter?	zhuh puh goo-tay?
tax	l'impôt m	añ-poh
taxi	le taxi	tak-see
tea	le thé	tay
herbal tea	la tisane	tee-zan
teacher	le professeur	pro-feh-sur
telephone	le téléphone	tay-lay-fon
telephone box	la cabine téléphonique	ka-been tay-lay-fo-neek
telephone call	le coup de téléphone	koo tay-lay-fon
telephone card	la télécarte	tay-lay-kart
telephone number	le numéro de téléphone	new-may-roh duh tay-lay-fon
to telephone	téléphoner	tay-lay-fo-nay
television	la télévision	tay-lay-vee-zyoñ
temperature	la température	tahñ-pay-ra-tewr
to have a temperature	avoir de la fièvre	a-vwar duh la fyevr
tennis	le tennis	the-nees
tent	la tente	tahñt
to text	envoyer un SMS à	ahñ-wa-yay uñ nes-em-es a
I'll text you	je t'enverrai un SMS	zhuh tahñ-veh-ray uñ nes-em-es
than	que	kuh
to thank	remercier	ruh-mehr-syay
thank you	merci	mehr-see
thank you very much	merci beaucoup	mehr-see boh-koo
that	cela/ça	suh-la/sa
that one	celui-là/celle-là	suh-lwee-la/sel-la
the	le/la/l'/les	luh/la/l'/lay

English – French

English – French

theatre	le théâtre	tay-atr
their	leur(s)	lur
them	eux	uh
there	là	la
there is/are...	il y a...	eel ya...
these	ces	say
these (ones)	ceux-ci/celles-ci	suh-see/sel-see
they	ils/elles	eel/el
thing	la chose	shohz
my things	mes affaires	may za-fehr
to think	penser	paññ-say
thirsty:		
I'm thirsty	j'ai soif	zhay swaf
this	ce/ceci	suh/suh-see
this one	celui-ci/ celle-ci	suh-lwee-see/ sel-see
those	ces	say
those (ones)	ceux-là/celles-là	suh-la/sel-la
throat	la gorge	gorzh
through	à travers	a tra-vehr
Thursday	jeudi	zhuh-dee

ticket	le billet; le ticket	bee-yeh; tee-keh
a single ticket	un aller simple	uñ na-lay sañpl
a return ticket	un aller-retour	uñ na-lay ruh-toor
ticket office	le guichet	gee-shet
tie	la cravate	kra-vat
tight (fitting)	serré(e)	seh-ray
tights	le collant	ko-lañ
till (cash desk)	la caisse	kes
till (until)	jusqu'à	zhews-ka
till 2 o'clock	jusqu'à deux heures	zhews-ka duh zur
time	le temps	tañ
time (of day)	l'heure f	ur
this time	cette fois	set fwa
what time is it?	quelle heure est-il?	kel ur ay-teel?
timetable	l'horaire m	o-rehr
tip (to waiter, etc.)	le pourboire	poor-bwar
to tip (waiter, etc.)	donner un pourboire à	do-nay uñ poor-bwar a

English	French	Pronunciation
tired	fatigué(e)	fa-tee-gay
to	à	ah̃/oh
(with name of country)	en/au	ah̃/oh
to London	à Londres	a loñdr
to the airport	à l'aéroport	a la-ay-roh-por
to France	en France	ah̃ frah̃s
to Canada	au Canada	oh ka-na-da
toast (to eat)	le pain grillé; le toast	pañ gree-yay; tost
today	aujourd'hui	oh-zhoor-dwee
toilet	les toilettes	twa-let
toll (motorway)	le péage	pay-azh
tomato	la tomate	to-mat
tomorrow	demain	duh-mañ
tomorrow morning	demain matin	duh-mañ ma-tañ
tonight	ce soir	se swar
too (also)	aussi	oh-see
it's too big	c'est trop grand	say troh grah̃
it's too hot	il fait trop chaud	eel feh troh shoh

English	French	Pronunciation
it's too noisy	il y a trop de bruit	eel ya troh duh bwee
tooth	la dent	dah̃
I have toothache	j'ai mal aux dents	zhay mal oh dah̃
toothbrush	la brosse à dents	bros a dah̃
toothpaste	le dentifrice	dah̃-tee-frees
top:		
the top floor	le dernier étage	dehr-nyay ay-tazh
top (of pyjamas, bikini, etc.)	le haut	oh
on top of (of hill, mountain)	le sommet	so-meh
total (amount)	sur	sewr
	le total	to-tal
tour	l'excursion f	ek-skewr-syoñ
tourist	le/la touriste	too-reest
tourist (information) office	le syndicat d'initiative/ l'office de/ du tourisme	sañ-dee-ka dee-nee-sya-teev/ o-fees duh/ dew too-reesm
towel	la serviette	sehr-vyet

English – French

English – French

town	la ville	veel	
town centre	le centre-ville	sahñtr-veel	
town hall	la mairie	meh-ree	
town plan	le plan de la ville	plañ duh la veel	
traffic	la circulation	seer-kewla-syoñ	
traffic jam	l'embouteillage *m*	añ-boo-tay-yazh	
traffic lights	les feux	fuh	
train	le train	trañ	
by train	par le train	par luh trañ	
the next train	le prochain train	pro-shañ trañ	
tram	le tramway	tram-way	
to translate	traduire	tra-dweer	
to travel	voyager	wa-ya-zhay	
travel agent's	l'agence de voyages *f*	a-zhañs duh wa-yazh	
tree	l'arbre *m*	arbr	
trip	l'excursion *f*	ek-skewr-syoñ	
trolley	le chariot	sha-ryoh	

to try; to try on (clothes, shoes)	essayer	eh-say-yay	
Tuesday	mardi	mar-dee	
tunnel	le tunnel	tew-nel	
to turn off (engine)	éteindre	ay-tañdr	
	couper	koo-pay	
to turn on (light, etc.)	allumer	a-lew-may	
(engine)	mettre en marche	metr añ marsh	
twin-bedded room	la chambre à deux lits	shahñbr a duh lee	
tyre	le pneu	pnuh	
U			
umbrella	le parapluie	pa-ra-plwee	
uncle	l'oncle *m*	oñkl	
uncomfortable	inconfortable	añ-koñ-for-tabl	
under	sous	soo	

English	French	Pronunciation
underground (train)	le métro	may-troh
to understand	comprendre	koñ-prahñdr
I don't understand	je ne comprends pas	zhuh nuh koñ-prahñ pa
do you understand?	vous comprenez?	voo koñ-pruh-nay?
unemployed	au chômage	oh shoh-mazh
United Kingdom	le Royaume-Uni	rwa-yohm ew-nee
United States	les États-Unis	ay-ta-zew-nee
university	l'université f	ew-nee-vehr-see-tay
unleaded	l'essence sans plomb f	eh-sahñs sahñ ploñ
upstairs	en haut	ahñ oh
urgent	urgent(e)	ewr-zhahñ(t)
us	nous	noo
useful	utile	ew-teel
usual	habituel(-elle)	a-bee-tew-el

	libre	leebr
	les vacances	va-kahñs
	valable	va-labl
	les objets de valeur	ob-zheh duh va-lur
	la TVA	tay-vay-a
	végétalien(ne)	vay-zhay-ta-lyañ/lyen
	les légumes	lay lay-gewm
	végétarien(ne)	vay-zhay-ta-ryañ/ryen
	très	treh
	la caméscope	ka-may-skop
	le village	vee-lazh
	le vinaigre	vee-negr
	le virus	vee-rews
	le visa	vee-za
	le séjour	say-zhoor
	visiter	vee-zee-tay

V

English	French
vacant	
vacation	
valid (ticket, driving licence, etc.)	
valuables	
VAT	
vegan	
vegetables	
vegetarian	
very	
video camera	
village	
vinegar	
virus	
visa	
visit	
to visit	

English – French

English – French

English	French	Pronunciation
visitor	le/la visiteur (-euse)	vee-zee-tur/tuhz
voicemail	la messagerie vocale	meh-sa-zhree vo-kal
W		
to wait for	attendre	a-tahñdr
waiter/	le/la serveur (-euse)	sehr-vur/sehr-vuhz
waitress		
waiting room	la salle d'attente	sal da-tahñt
to wake up	se réveiller	suh ray-vay-yay
Wales	le pays de Galles	pay-yee duh gal
walk: to go for a walk	faire une promenade	fehr wun prom-nad
to walk	aller à pied; marcher	a-lay a pyay; mar-shay
wall	le mur	mewr
wallet	le portefeuille	port-fuh-yuh
I want...	je veux...	zhuh vuh...
we want...	nous voulons...	noo voo-loñ...
warm	chaud(e)	shoh(d)
it's warm (weather)	il fait bon	eel feh boñ
it's too warm	il fait trop chaud	eel feh troh shoh
washing machine	la machine à laver	ma-sheen a la-vay
washing powder	la lessive	leh-seev
washing-up liquid	le produit pour la vaisselle	pro-dwee poor la vay-sel
watch	la montre	moñtr
to watch (look at)	regarder	ruh-gar-day
water	l'eau f	oh
drinking water	l'eau potable	oh po-tabl
sparkling mineral water	l'eau minérale gazeuse	oh mee-nay-ral ga-zuhz
still mineral water	l'eau minérale plate	oh mee-nay-ral plat
watermelon	la pastèque	pas-tek
way (manner)	la manière	ma-nyehr
(route)	le chemin	shuh-mañ

English	French	
way in (entrance)	l'entrée *f*	lahñ-tray
way out (exit)	la sortie	sor-tee
we	nous	noo
to wear	porter	por-tay
weather	le temps	tahñ
weather forecast	la météo	ma-ytay-oh
Wednesday	mercredi	mehr-kruh-dee
week	la semaine	suh-men
last week	la semaine dernière	suh-men dehr-nyehr
next week	la semaine prochaine	suh-men pro-shen
per week	par semaine	par suh-men
this week	cette semaine	set suh-men
weekend	le week-end	wee-kend
well (healthy)	en bonne santé	ahñ bon sahñ-tay
he's not well	il est souffrant	eel ay soo-frahñ
I'm very well	je vais très bien	zhuh veh treh byañ
well done (steak)	bien cuit(e)	byañ kwee(t)

English – French

Welsh	gallois(e)	ga-lwa(z)			
west	l'ouest *m*	oo-est			
wet	mouillé(e)	moo-yay			
what	que; quel/quelle; quoi	kuh; kel; kwa			
what is it?	qu'est-ce que c'est?	kes kuh say?			
wheelchair	le fauteuil roulant	foh-tuh-yuh roo-lahñ			
when	quand	kahñ			
(at what time?)	à quelle heure?	a kel ur			
when is it?	c'est quand?; c'est à quelle heure?	say kahñ?; say ta kel ur?			
where	où	oo			
where is it?	c'est où?	say oo?			
where is the hotel?	où est l'hôtel?	oo ay loh-tel?			
which	quel/quelle	kel			
which (one)?	lequel/laquelle?	luh-kel/la-kel?			

English – French

which (ones)?	lesquels/ lesquelles?	lay-kel?	without milk/ sugar	sans lait/ sucre	sahñ leh/ sewkr
white	blanc (blanche)	blahñ(sh)	woman	la femme	fam
who	qui	kee	wool	la laine	len
who is it?	qui c'est?	kee say?	word	le mot	moh
whose:			work	le travail	tra-va-yuh
whose is it?	c'est à qui?	say ta kee?	to work (person)	travailler	tra-va-yay
why	pourquoi	poor-kwa	(machine, car)	fonctionner;	foñ-ksyo-nay;
wife	la femme	fam		marcher	mar-shay
window	la fenêtre	fuh-netr	it doesn't work	ça ne marche	sa nuh marsh
(shop)	la vitrine	vee-treen		pas	pa
wine	le vin	vañ	to write	écrire	ay-kreer
wine list	la carte des vins	kart day vañ	please write it	vous me	voo muh
winter	l'hiver m	ee-vehr	down	l'écrivez, s'il	lay-kree-vay seel
with	avec	a-vek		vous plaît?	voo pleh?
with ice	avec des glaçons	a-vek day gla-soñ	wrong	faux (fausse)	foh(s)
with milk/	avec du lait/	a-vek dew leh/			
sugar	sucre	sewkr	X		
without	sans	soñ	X-ray	la radio(graphie)	ra-dyoh (gra-fee)
without ice	sans glaçons	sahñ gla-soñ	to X-ray	faire une radio	fehr ewn ra-dyoh
				(graphie)	(gra-fee)

Y

year	l'an *m*; l'année *f*	ahñ; la-nay
this year	cette année	set a-nay
next year	l'année prochaine	a-nay pro-shen
last year	l'année dernière	a-nay dehr-nyehr
yellow	jaune	zhohn
Yellow Pages	les pages jaunes	pazh zhohn
yes	oui	wee
yes please	oui, merci	wee, mehr-see
yesterday	hier	ee-yehr
yet: not yet	pas encore	pa (z)ahñ-kor
yoghurt	le yaourt	ya-oort
plain yoghurt	le yaourt nature	ya-oort na-tewr
you (familiar)	tu	tew
(polite)	vous	voo
young	jeune	zhuhn
your (familiar singular)	ton/ta	toñ/ta
(familiar plural)	tes	tay
(polite singular)	votre	votr
(polite plural)	vos	voh

Z

zero	le zéro	zay-roh
zip	la fermeture éclair	fehr-muh-tewr ay-klehr
zoo	le zoo	zoh

English – French

French – English

A

French	English
à	to; at
accès interdit *m*	no entry
accident *m*	accident
accueil *m*	reception; information
acheter	to buy
addition *f*	bill
adresse *f*	address
adressez-vous à	enquire at (*office*)
aérogare *f*	terminal
aéroport *m*	airport
affaires *fpl*	business; belongings
bonne affaire	bargain
affiche *f*	poster; notice
âge *m*	age
du troisième âge	senior citizen
âgé(e)	elderly
âgé de... ans	aged ... years
agence *f*	agency; branch
agence de voyages	travel agency
agence immobilière	estate agent's
agent de police *m*	police officer
aider	to help
aimer	to enjoy; to love (*person*)
aire: *aire de jeux*	play area
aire de repos	rest area
aire de service	service area
aire de stationnement	layby
alcool *m*	alcohol; fruit brandy
algues *fpl*	seaweed
allégé(e)	low-fat
Allemagne *f*	Germany
allemand(e)	German
aller	to go
aller (simple) *m*	single ticket
aller-retour *m*	return ticket
allumé(e)	on (*light*)
allumez vos phares	switch on headlights
alpinisme *m*	mountaineering
alsacien(ne)	Alsatian
ambassade *f*	embassy
ambulance *f*	ambulance
américain(e)	American
Amérique *f*	America
ami(e) *m/f*	friend
petit(e) ami(e)	boyfriend/girlfriend
amour *m*	love
ampoule *f*	blister; light bulb
an *m*	year
Nouvel An m	New Year

French	English
analgésique m	painkiller
ancien(ne)	old; former
angine f	tonsillitis
Anglais m	Englishman
anglais m	English (language)
anglais(e)	English
Angleterre f	England
animal m	animal
animal domestique	pet
année f	year; vintage
anniversaire m	anniversary; birthday
annonce f	advertisement
annulation f	cancellation
anti-insecte m	insect repellent
antibiotique m	antibiotic
antihistamine m	antihistamine
antimoustique m	mosquito repellent
août	August
appareil m	appliance; camera
appareil acoustique	hearing aid
appareil photo	camera
appeler	to call (speak, phone)
appeler en PVC	to reverse the charges
appuyer	to press
après	after
après-midi m	afternoon
arbre m	tree
argent m	money; silver
argent liquide	cash
arrêt m	bus stop
arrêt d'autobus	bus stop
arrêter	to arrest; to stop
arrêter le moteur	to turn off the engine
arrêtez!	stop!
arrivées fpl	arrivals
arriver	to arrive; to happen
arrondissement m	district
article m	item; article
articles de toilette	toiletries
ascenseur m	lift
assez	enough; quite (rather)
assiette f	plate
assurance f	insurance
assuré(e)	insured
assurer	to assure; to insure
asthme m	asthma
atelier m	workshop; artist's studio
attacher	to fasten (seatbelt)

French – English

French – English

French	English
attendre	to wait (for)
attention!	look out!
faire attention	to be careful
au lieu de	instead of
au revoir	goodbye
auberge *f*	inn
auberge de jeunesse	youth hostel
aujourd'hui	today
aussi	also
autobus *m*	bus
automne *m*	autumn
autoroute *f*	motorway
autre	other
autres directions	other routes
avance: *à l'avance*	in advance
avant	before
avec	with
avion *m*	aeroplane
avis *m*	notice; warning
avoir	to have
avril	April
B	
bagages *mpl*	luggage
bagages à main	hand luggage
baie *f*	bay *(along coast)*
baignade interdite	no bathing/ swimming
bain *m*	bath *(act of bathing)*
bal *m*	ball; dance
balade *f*	walk; drive; trek
balcon *m*	balcony; circle *(theatre)*; balcony
ball-trap *m*	clay pigeon shooting
balle *f*	ball *(small, e.g. golf, tennis)*
ballon *m*	balloon; ball *(large)*; brandy or large wine glass
banane *f*	banana; bumbag
banc *m*	seat; bench
banlieue *f*	suburbs
banque *f*	bank
bar *m*	bar
barbe à papa *f*	candy floss
barque *f*	rowing boat
barrage routier	road block
route barrée	road closed
bas *m*	bottom *(of page, etc.)*; stocking
en bas	below; downstairs
bas(se)	low
bateau *m*	boat; ship
bâtiment *m*	building
bâton (de ski) *m*	ski pole

beau (belle) — lovely; handsome; beautiful; nice (enjoyable)

beaucoup (de) — much/many; a lot of

bébé m — baby

belge — Belgian

Belgique f — Belgium

besoin: avoir besoin de — to need

bibliothèque f — library

bien — well; right; good (steak, etc.)

bien cuit(e) — well done (steak, etc.)

bientôt — soon; shortly

bienvenu(e) — welcome!

bière f — beer

bière (à la) pression — draught beer

bière blonde — lager

bière brune — bitter

bijouterie f — jeweller's; jewellery

billet m — note; ticket

billet aller-retour — return ticket

billet d'avion — plane ticket

billet de banque — banknote

billet simple — one-way ticket

biologique — organic

blanc (blanche) — white; blank

blessé(e) — injured

bleu m — bruise

bleu(e) — blue; very rare (steak, etc.)

boire — to drink

bois m — wood

boisson f — drink

boisson non alcoolisée — soft drink

boîte f — can; box

boîte à lettres — post box

boîte de nuit — night club

bol m — bowl (for soup, etc.)

bon m — token; voucher

bon (bonne) — good; right; nice

bon marché — inexpensive

bonbon m — sweet

bonsoir — good evening

bord m — border; edge; verge

à bord — on board

au bord de la mer — at the seaside

bouche f — mouth

boucherie f — butcher's shop

bouée de sauvetage f — life belt

boulangerie f — bakery

French – English

French – English

boules *fpl*	game similar to bowls	**brun(e)**	brown; dark	**cadeau** *m*	gift
Bourgogne	Burgundy	**bureau** *m*	desk; office	**café** *m*	coffee; café
bout *m*	end	**bureau de change**	foreign exchange office	*café au lait*	white coffee
bouteille *f*	bottle			*café crème*	creamy coffee
bouton *m*	button; switch; spot	**bureau de poste**	post office	*café noir*	black coffee
bouton de fièvre	cold sore	*bureau de renseignements*	information office	**caisse** *f*	cash desk; case
bras *m*	arm	**bureau des objets trouvés**	lost-property office	**calmant** *m*	sedative
brasserie *f*	café; brewery			**camping** *m*	camping; campsite
Bretagne *f*	Brittany	**bus** *m*	bus		
breton(ne)	from Brittany	**butane** *m*	camping gas	**Canada** *m*	Canada
britannique	British			**canadien(ne)**	Canadian
brocante *f*	second-hand goods; flea market	**C**		**canapé** *m*	sofa; open sandwich
		ça	that	*canapé-lit*	sofa bed
		ça va	it's OK; I'm OK	**canne à pêche**	fishing rod
brouillard *m*	fog	*ça va?*	are you OK?	**canot de sauvetage**	lifeboat
brûlé(e)	burnt	**cabine** *f*	beach hut; cubicle	**car** *m*	coach
brûlures d'estomac *fpl*	heartburn	*cabine d'essayage*	changing room	**carrefour** *m*	crossroads

French	English
carte f	map; card; menu; pass (bus, train)
carte bleue	credit card
carte d'abonnement	season ticket
carte d'embarquement	boarding card/pass
carte d'identité	identity card
carte de crédit	credit card
carte des vins	wine list
carte postale	postcard
carte routière	road map
carte vermeille	senior citizen's rail pass
casque m	helmet
casque (à écouteurs)	headphones
cassé(e)	broken
casse-croûte m	snacks
cause f	cause

French	English
caution f	security (for loan); deposit
caution à verser	deposit required
cave f	cellar
ceci	this
cédez le passage	give way
ceinture de sécurité	seatbelt
cela	that
célèbre	famous
cent m	hundred
centre m	centre
centre commercial	shopping centre
centre de loisirs	leisure centre
centre équestre	riding school
centre-ville m	city centre
cercle m	circle; ring
céréales fpl	cereal

French	English
cette	this; that
CFF mpl	Swiss Railways
chacun(e)	each
chaîne f	chain; channel; (mountain) range
chaise f	chair
chaise de bébé f	high chair
chambre f	bedroom; room
chambre d'hôte	bed and breakfast
chambres	rooms to let (on sign)
champ m	field
champ de courses	racecourse
champignon vénéneux m	toadstool
chance f	luck
chantier m	building site; roadworks

French – English

French – English

chaque	each; every	
charbon de bois	charcoal	
charcuterie f	pork butcher's; delicatessen; cooked meat	
chariot m	trolley	
chasse f	hunting; shooting	
chasse gardée	private hunting	
château m	castle; mansion	
chaud(e)	hot	
chauffage m	heating	
chaussée déformée	uneven road surface	
chaussée rétrécie	road narrows	
chaussée verglacée	icy road	
chaussette f	sock	
chaussure f	shoe; boot	
chef de train	train guard	

chemin m	path; lane; track; way	
chemin de fer	railway	
chemise f	shirt	
chemisier m	blouse	
chèque de voyage	traveller's cheque	
cher (chère)	dear; expensive	
cheval m	horse	
faire du cheval	to ride	
cheveux mpl	hair	
chez	at the house of	
chez moi	at my home	
choix m	range; choice; selection	
chose f	thing	
cimetière f	cemetery; graveyard	
circuit m	round trip; circuit	
circulation f	traffic	

cirque m	circus	
cité f	city; housing estate	
clair(e)	clear; light	
classe f	grade; class	
clé f	key; spanner	
clef f	key	
client(e) m/f	client; customer	
climatisation f	air-conditioning	
climatisé(e)	air-conditioned	
cocher	to 'tick' *(on form – in fact, you must cross)*	
code postal	postcode	
code secret	pin number	
cœur m	heart	
coffre-fort m	safe	
coiffeur m	hairdresser; barber	
coiffeuse f	hairdresser	
coin m	corner	

French	English
col m	collar; pass (in mountains)
combien	how much/many
combinaison de plongée f	wetsuit
comme	like
comme ça	like this; like that
commencer	to begin
comment	how
comment?	pardon?
commissariat (de police) m	police station
communication f	communication; call (on telephone)
compartiment m	compartment (train)
complet(-ète)	full (up)
composer	to dial (a number)
composter votre billet	validate your ticket
comprenant	including
comprimé m	tablet
compris(e)	included
non compris	not included
comptant m	cash
compte m	number; account
compte en banque	bank account
comptoir m	counter (in shop, bar, etc.)
concierge m/f	caretaker; janitor
concours m	contest; aid
conduire	to drive
confirmer	to confirm
congélateur m	freezer
conserver	to keep; to retain (ticket, etc.)
consigne f	deposit; left luggage
consommation f	drink
contenu m	contents
continuer	to continue
contraceptif m	contraceptive
contrat m	contract
contrat de location	lease
contravention f	fine (penalty)
contre	against; versus
contrôle m	check
contrôle des passeports	passport control
contrôle radar	speed check
contrôleur (-euse) m/f	ticket inspector
cordonnerie f	shoe repairer's

French – English

French	English
corps m	body
correspondance f	connection (transport)
Corse f	Corsica
costume m	suit (man's)
côte f	coast; hill; rib
Côte d'Azur f	French Riviera
côté m	side
à côté de	beside; next to
coton m	cotton
couche (de bébé) f	nappy
couette f	continental quilt; duvet
couleur f	colour
couloir m	corridor; aisle
coup de soleil	sunburn
coup de téléphone	phone call
cour f	court; courtyard
courant m	power; current

French	English
courrier m	mail; post
courrier électronique	e-mail
cours m	lesson; course; rate
course f	race (sport); errand
course hippique	horse race
court(e)	short
coût m	cost
couteau m	knife
couvert m	cover charge; place setting
couvert(e)	covered
couverture f	blanket; cover
crémerie f	dairy
crêperie f	pancake shop/ restaurant
crise cardiaque	heart attack
croisement m	junction (road)

French	English
croisière f	cruise
croix f	cross
cru(e)	raw
cuiller/cuillère f	spoon
cuiller/cuillère à café	teaspoon
cuir m	leather
cuisine f	cooking; cuisine; kitchen
cuisine familiale	home cooking
cuisinière f	cook; cooker
cuit(e)	cooked
bien cuit(e)	well done (steak, etc.)
cyclisme m	cycling

D

French	English
dame f	lady
dames	ladies; ladies' (toilet)

danger *m*	danger	
dangereux (-euse)	dangerous	
dans	into; in; on	
date *f*	date (day)	
date de naissance	date of birth	
de	from; of; some	
débutant(e) *m/f*	beginner	
décaféiné(e)	decaffeinated	
décembre	December	
déclaration	declaration	
déclaration de douane	customs declaration	
décollage *m*	take-off (plane)	
décoller	to take off (plane)	
décrocher	to lift the receiver	
dedans	inside	
défectueux (-euse)	faulty	

défense de...	no.../ ... forbidden
défense de fumer	no smoking
défense de stationner	no parking
dégustation de vins	wine tasting
dehors	outside; outdoors
déjeuner *m*	lunch
délicieux (-euse)	delicious
délit *m*	offence
deltaplane *m*	hang-glider
demain	tomorrow
demande *f*	application; request
demander	to ask (for)
démarqué(e)	reduced (goods)
demi(e)	half

demi-pension *f*	half board
demi-tarif *m*	half fare
demi-tour *m*	U-turn
dent *m*	tooth
dentifrice *m*	toothpaste
départ *m*	departure
département *m*	county
dépasser	to exceed; to overtake
déranger	to disturb
dernier(-ère)	last; latest
derrière	at the back; behind
dès: *dès votre arrivée*	as soon as you arrive
désolée(e)	sorry
dessous: *en dessous de*	underneath
dessus: *au dessus de*	on top (of)

French – English

French – English

French	English
destination: *à destination de*	bound for
détourner	to divert
deux	two
deux fois	twice
les deux	both
deuxième m	second
devant m	front; in front (of)
déviation f	diversion
diabète m	diabetes
diarrhée f	diarrhoea
diététique: *produits diététiques*	health foods
difficile	difficult
dimanche m	Sunday
dîner m	dinner
dîner spectacle m	cabaret dinner
dire	to say; to tell
direct: *train direct*	through train
directeur m	manager; headmaster
disparu(e)	missing (disappeared)
disponible	available
distributeur automatique	vending machine; cash machine
divertissements mpl	entertainment
docteur m	doctor
domicile m	home; address
dormir	to sleep
douane f	customs
douche f	shower
douleur f	pain
douloureux (-euse)	painful
doux (douce)	mild; gentle; soft; sweet
douzaine f	dozen
drogue f	drug
droite(e)	right (not left); straight
à droite	on/to the right
tenez votre droite	keep to right
tout droit	straight on
dur(e)	hard; hard-boiled; tough

E

French	English
eau f	water
eau de javel	bleach
eau minérale	mineral water
eau potable	drinking water
échelle de secours	fire escape
écluse f	lock (in canal)

French	English
école f	school
écossais(e)	Scottish
Écosse f	Scotland
écouter	to listen to
écran solaire	sunscreen lotion
écran total	sunblock
écrire	to write
édulcorant m	sweetener
embarquement m	boarding
emporter: **à emporter**	take-away
en	some; any; in; to; made of
en cas de	in case of
en face de	opposite
en gros	in bulk; wholesale
en panne	out of order
en retard	late
en train	by train
enceinte	pregnant
encore	still; yet; again
enfant m/f	child
enregistrement m	check-in desk
enregistrer	to record; to check in; to video
ensemble	together
entracte m	interval
entre	between
entrée f	entrance; admission; starter (food)
entrée gratuite	admission free
entrée interdite	no entry
entrez!	come in!
environs mpl	surroundings
épicerie f	grocer's shop
épicerie fine	delicatessen
épuisé(e)	sold out; used up
équipage m	crew
équitation f	horse-riding
erreur f	mistake
escalade f	climbing
escalator m	escalator
escalier m	stairs
escalier de secours	fire escape
Espagne f	Spain
espagnol m	Spanish (language)
espagnol(e)	Spanish
essayer	to try; to try on
essence f	petrol
essence sans plomb	unleaded petrol
estomac m	stomach
et	and
étage m	storey
États-Unis	United States
été m	summer
éteindre	to turn off

French – English

French – English

éteint(e)	out (light)
étiquette f	label; tag
étranger(-ère) m/f	foreigner
être	to be
étroit(e)	narrow; tight
étudiant(e) m/f	student
européen(ne)	European
éviter	to avoid
exact(e)	right (correct)
excédent de bagages m	excess baggage
excès de vitesse m	speeding
exclu(e)	excluded
excursion f	trip; outing; excursion
excusez-moi!	excuse me!
exemplaire m	copy
exposition f	exhibition
extérieur(e)	outside
extra	top-quality; first-rate

F

fabriqué en…	made in…
face: en face (de)	opposite
facile	easy
facture f	invoice
faire	to make; to do
fait main	handmade
falaise f	cliff
famille f	family
farine f	flour
fatigué(e)	tired
fauteuil roulant m	armchair; seat wheelchair
faxer	to fax
femme f	woman; wife
femme de chambre	chambermaid
femme de ménage	cleaner
fenêtre f	window
fente f	crack; slot
fer m	iron
fer à repasser	iron (for clothes)
férié(e): jour férié m	public holiday
ferme f	farmhouse; farm
fermé(e)	closed
fermer	to close/shut; to turn off
fermer à clé	to lock
ferry m	car ferry
fête f	holiday; fête; party
fête foraine	funfair
feu m	fire; traffic lights
février	February
fièvre: avoir de la fièvre	to have a temperature

file f	lane; row
filet m	net; filet (of meat, fish)
fille f	daughter; girl
fils m	son
fin f	end
fin(e)	thin (material); fine (delicate)
fini(e)	finished
finir	to end; to finish
fleur f	flower
fleuriste m/f	florist
fleuve m	river
foire f	fair
fois f	time (occasion)
cette fois	this time
une fois	once
foncé(e)	dark (colour)
fonctionner	to work (machine)

fond m	back (of hall, room); bottom
forêt f	forest
forfait m	fixed price; ski pass
forme f	shape; style
formulaire m	form (document)
four m	oven
frais, fraîche	fresh; cool; wet (paint)
français m	French (language)
français(e)	French
frère m	brother
frigo m	fridge
froid(e)	cold
frontière f	border; boundary
fruit m	fruit
fumer	to smoke
fumeurs	smokers

G

gagner	to earn; to win
galerie f	art gallery; arcade; roof-rack
galloise(e)	Welsh
garage m	garage
garantie f	guarantee
garçon m	boy; waiter
gare f	railway station
gare routière	bus terminal
gasoil, gaz-oil m	diesel fuel
gauche	left
à gauche	to/on the left
gazeux(-euse)	fizzy
gelé(e)	frozen
gendarme m	policeman (in rural areas)
gendarmerie f	police station
gilet m	waistcoat

232 | 233

French – English

French – English

French	English
gilet de sauvetage	life jacket
gîte m	self-catering house/flat
glace f	ice; ice cream; mirror
glacière f	cool-box (for picnic)
glissant(e)	slippery
gorge f	throat; gorge
goût m	flavour; taste
grand(e)	great; high (speed, number); big; tall
grand-mère f	grandmother
grand-père m	grandfather
Grande-Bretagne f	Great Britain
gras(se)	fat; greasy
gratis, gratuit(e)	free (of charge)
grave	serious
grippe f	flu
gris(e)	grey
gros(se)	big; large; fat
grotte f	cave
guerre f	war
guichet m	ticket office; counter
guide m	guide; guidebook
guide de conversation	phrase book

H

French	English
habiter	to live (in)
halles fpl	covered food market
handicapé(e)	disabled (person)
haut m	top (of ladder, bikini)
en haut	upstairs
haut(e)	high; tall
hauteur f	height
hébergement m	lodging
herbe f	grass
heure f	hour; time of day
heure de pointe	rush hour
hier	yesterday
hippisme m	horse riding
hippodrome m	racecourse
hiver m	winter
hollandais(e)	Dutch
homme m	man
honoraires mpl	fee
hôpital m	hospital
horaire m	timetable; schedule
hors: hors de	out of
hors-saison	off-season
hors service	out of order

hors-taxe	duty-free	
hôte m	host; guest	
hôtel m	hotel	
hôtel de ville m	town hall	
hôtesse f	stewardess	
huile f	oil	
hypermarché m	hypermarket	

ici	here
il y a...	there is/are...
il y a une semaine	there's a fault
il y a un défaut	a week ago
il y a	ago
île f	island
immeuble m	building (offices, flats)
impasse f	dead end
imperméable m	waterproof
incendie m	fire

inclus(e)	included; inclusive
indicatif m	dialling code
indigestion f	indigestion
infirmier(-ière) m/f	infirmary nurse
informations f pl	news; information
inondation f	flood
instant m	moment
un instant!	just a minute!
institut de beauté	beauty salon
interdit	forbidden
intéressant(e)	interesting
intérieur: **à l'intérieur**	indoors
introduire	to introduce; to insert
invité(e) m/f	guest

irlandaise(e)	Irish
Irlande f	Ireland
Irlande du Nord f	Northern Ireland
issue de secours f	emergency exit
itinéraire m	route
itinéraire touristique	scenic route

J

jamais	never
jambe f	leg
janvier	January
Japon m	Japan
jardin m	garden
jaune	yellow
jeton m	token
jeu m	game; set (of tools, etc); gambling

French – English

French – English

jeudi *m*	Thursday
jeune	young
joli(e)	pretty
jouer	to play (games)
jouet *m*	toy
jour *m*	day
jour férié	public holiday
journal *m*	newspaper
journée *f*	day (length of time)
juif (juive)	Jewish
juillet	July
juin	June
jumelles *fpl*	twins; binoculars
jus *m*	juice
jus d'orange	orange juice
jus de fruit	fruit juice
jusqu'à/au/aux	until; till

K

kas(c)her	kosher
kilométrage illimité	unlimited mileage
kilomètre *m*	kilometre
kiosque *m*	kiosk; newsstand
klaxonner	to sound one's horn

L

là	there
lac *m*	lake
laine *f*	wool
laissez en blanc	leave blank
lait *m*	milk
lait cru	unpasteurised milk
lait *démaquillant*	make-up remover

lait demi-écrémé	semi-skimmed milk
lait écrémé	skim(med) milk
lait entier	full-cream milk
lait longue conservation	long-life milk
lait maternisé	baby milk; formula
lait solaire	suntan lotion
lames de rasoir	razor blades
langue *f*	tongue; language
lavable	washable
lavage *m*	washing
lave-linge *m*	washing machine
laver	to wash
se laver	to wash (oneself)
laverie automatique *f*	launderette

French	English
leçon f	lesson
leçons particulières	private lessons
légume m	vegetable
lent(e)	slow
lentement	slowly
lentille f	lentil; lens (of glasses)
lentille de contact	contact lens
lessive f	soap powder; washing
lettre f	letter
leur(s)	their
lèvre f	lip
librairie f	bookshop
libre	free; vacant
libre-service	self-service
lieu m	place (location)
ligne f	line; service; route
limitation de vitesse f	speed limit
lin m	linen (cloth)
linge m	linen (bed, table); laundry
lingettes fpl	baby wipes
liste f	list
lit m	bed
livre f	pound
livre m	book
location f	hiring (out); letting
logement m	accommodation
loi f	law
loin	far
Londres	London
long(ue)	long
le long de	along
longtemps	for a long time
louer	to let; to hire; to rent
à louer	for hire/to rent
lourd(e)	heavy
lumière f	light
lundi m	Monday
lune de miel	honeymoon
lunettes fpl	glasses
lunettes de soleil	sunglasses
lunettes protectrices/ de protection	goggles
M	M
machine à laver	washing machine
magasin m	shop
grand magasin	department store
mai	May

French - English

maillot de bain *m*	swimsuit
main *f*	hand
maintenant	now
mairie *f*	town hall
maison *f*	house; home
maison de campagne	villa
mal	badly
mal *m*	harm; pain
mal de dents	toothache
mal de mer	seasickness
mal de tête	headache
faire du mal à quelqu'un	to harm someone
malade	ill; sick
malade *m/f*	sick person; patient
maladie *f*	disease
Manche *f*	the Channel
manger	to eat

marchand *m*	dealer; merchant
marché *m*	market
marché aux puces	flea market
marcher	to walk; to work (machine, car)
en marche	on (machine)
mardi *m*	Tuesday
mardi gras	Shrove Tuesday
marée *f*	tide
marée basse	low tide
marée haute	high tide
mari *m*	husband
marié(e)	married
marionnette *f*	puppet
marron	brown
mars	March
matelas *m*	mattress
matériel *m*	equipment; kit
matin *m*	morning

mécanicien *m*	mechanic
médecin *m*	doctor
médicament *m*	medicine; drug; medication
Méditerranée *f*	Mediterranean Sea
meilleur(e)	best; better
mél *m*	e-mail
membre *m*	member (of club, etc.)
même	same
méningite *f*	meningitis
menu *m*	set menu
mer *f*	sea
merci	thank you
mercredi *m*	Wednesday
mère *f*	mother
message *m*	message
messe *f*	mass (church)

French – English

messieurs *mpl*	men; gentlemen; gents' (toilet)	minute *f*	minute	monsieur *m*	gentleman
mesure *f*	measurement	miroir *m*	mirror	Monsieur *m*	Mr; Sir
météo *f*	weather forecast	mistral *m*	strong cold dry wind (*South of France*)	montagne *f*	mountain
métier *m*	trade; occupation			monter à cheval	to horse-ride
métro *m*	underground	mixte	mixed	morceau *m*	piece; bit; cut (*of meat*)
mettre en marche	to turn on	mode d'emploi	instructions for use	morsure *f*	bite
meublé(e)	furnished	moins	less; minus	mot *m*	word; note (*letter*)
meubles *mpl*	furniture	*moins (de)*	less (than)	*mot de passe*	password
midi *m*	midday; noon	*moins cher*	cheaper	moteur *m*	engine; motor
Midi *m*	the south of France	mois *m*	month	moto *f*	motorbike
mieux	better; best	moitié *f*	half	mouchoir *m*	handkerchief
mille *m*	thousand	*à moitié prix*	half-price	moustique *m*	mosquito
millimètre *m*	millimetre	mon/ma/mes	my	moyen(ne)	average
mineur(e)	under age; minor	monde *m*	world	mur *m*	wall
minuit *m*	midnight	moniteur *m*	instructor; coach	mûr(e)	mature; ripe
		monitrice *f*	instructress; coach	musée *m*	museum
		monnaie *f*	currency; change	*musée d'art*	art gallery
				Musulman(e)	Muslim

French – English

N

French	English
natation f	swimming
nature f	wildlife
naturel(le)	natural
navette f	shuttle (bus service)
navigation f	sailing
négatif m	negative (photography)
neige f	snow
nettoyage m	cleaning
nettoyage à sec	dry-cleaning
neuf (neuve)	new
névralgie f	headache
nez m	nose
Noël m	Christmas
noir(e)	black
nom m	name; noun
nom de famille	family name
nom de jeune fille	maiden name
nombre m	number
nombreux (-euse)	numerous
non	no; not
non alcoolisé(e)	non-alcoholic
non-fumeur	non-smoking
nord m	north
normal(e)	normal; standard (size)
nos	our
note f	note; bill; memo
notre	our
nourriture f	food
nouveau (nouvelle)	new
de nouveau	again
novembre	November
nuageux(-euse)	cloudy
nuit f	night
bonne nuit	good night
numéro m	number; act; issue

O

French	English
objectif m	objective; lens (of camera)
objet m	object
objets de valeur	valuable items
objets trouvés	lost property
obligatoire	compulsory
obtenir	to get; to obtain
occasion f	occasion; bargain
occupé(e)	busy; hired (taxi); engaged
octobre	October
office m	service (church); office
office de/du tourisme	tourist office
offre f	offer

French	English
œil m	eye
or m	gold
orange	orange; amber (traffic light)
orchestre m	orchestra; stalls (in theatre)
ordinaire	ordinary
ordinateur m	computer
ordonnance f	prescription
ordre m	order
à l'ordre de	payable to
oreille f	ear
ou	or
où	where
oublier	to forget
ouest m	west
oui	yes
ouvert(e)	open; on (tap, gas, etc.)
ouvrir	to open

P

French	English
page f	page
pages jaunes	Yellow Pages
palais m	palace
panier m	basket
panne f	breakdown
panneau m	sign
pansement m	bandage
papier m	paper
papier cadeau	gift-wrap
papier hygiénique	toilet paper
papiers	identity papers; (vehicle) documents
par exemple	for example
par jour	per day
par téléphone	by phone
parc m	park
parc d'attractions	funfair

French	English
parce que	because
parcmètre m	parking meter
pardon!	sorry!; excuse me!
parent(e) m/f	relative
parfait(e)	perfect
parfum m	perfume; flavour
parfumerie f	perfume shop
parking m	car park
parking souterrain	underground car park
parking surveillé	attended car park
parler (à)	to speak (to)
partie f	part; match (game)
partir	to leave; to go
à partir de	from
partout	everywhere
pas	not

French – English

French – English

passage *m*	passage
passage à niveau	level crossing
passage clouté	pedestrian crossing
passage interdit	no through way
passage souterrain	underpass
passager (-ère) *m/f*	passenger
passeport *m*	passport
passer	to pass; to spend (time)
se passer	to happen
passerelle *f*	gangway (bridge)
passe-temps *m*	hobby
pastille *f*	lozenge
patins à glace *m*	ice skates
patins à roulettes	roller skates

patinoire *f*	skating rink
pâtisserie *f*	cake shop; little cake
payer	to pay (for)
payé(e)	paid
payé(e) d'avance	prepaid
pays *m*	land; country
du pays	local
Pays-Bas *mpl*	Netherlands
Pays de Galles *m*	Wales
péage *m*	toll (motorway, etc.)
peau *f*	skin; hide (leather)
pêche *f*	peach; fishing
pêcher	to fish
pédalo *m*	pedal boat/pedalo
pelote *f*	ball

pelote basque	pelota (ball game for two players)
pendant	during
pendant que	while
pension *f*	guesthouse
pension complète	full board
pente *f*	slope
perdre	to lose
perdu(e)	lost (object)
père *m*	father
périmé(e)	out of date; expired
périphérique *m*	ring road
permis *m*	permit; licence
permis de chasse	hunting permit
permis de conduire	driving licence
permis de pêche	fishing permit
personne *f*	person

French – English

French	English
pétanque f	type of bowls
petit(e)	small; slight
petit déjeuner m	breakfast
peu	little; few
à peu près	approximately
un peu (de)	a bit (of)
phare m	headlight; lighthouse
pharmacie f	chemist's; pharmacy
pichet m	jug; carafe
pièce f	room (in house); play (theatre); coin
pièce d'identité	means of identification
pièce de rechange	spare part
pied m	foot
à pied	on foot
piéton m	pedestrian
pile f	pile; battery
pilule f	(contraceptive) pill
piquet m	peg (for tent)
piqûre f	insect bite; injection; sting
piscine f	swimming pool
piste de luge	ski-run; runway; toboggan run
piste pour débutants	nursery slope
placard m	cupboard
place f	square (in town); seat; space (room)
plage f	beach
plainte f	complaint
plaisir m	enjoyment; pleasure
plaît; s'il vous/ te plaît	please
plan m	map (of town); street map
plan de la ville	street map
planche f	plank; ironing board
planche à repasser	ironing board
planche à voile	sailboard(ing); windsurfer/ing
planche de surf	surfboard
plat m	dish; course (of meal); main course
plat principal	main course
plein(e) (de)	full (of)
le plein!	fill it up! (car)
plein tarif	peak rate; full fare
pleuvoir	to rain
il pleut	it's raining
plonger	to dive

French – English

French	English
pluie f	rain
plus	more; most
plus grand(e) (que)	bigger (than)
plus tard	later
pneu m	tyre
pneu crevé	burst tyre
pneu dégonflé	flat tyre
poche f	pocket
poêle f	frying pan
poids m	weight
poids lourd	heavy goods vehicle
point m	place; point; stitch; dot
pointure f	size (of shoes)
poison m	poison
poissonnerie f	fishmonger's shop
police f	policy (insurance); police
pompiers mpl	fire brigade
pont m	bridge; deck (of ship)
portable m	mobile phone; laptop
porte f	door; gate
portefeuille m	wallet
porter	to wear; to carry
porte-clefs m	keyring
porte-monnaie m	purse
poste f	post; post office
poste de contrôle	checkpoint
poste de secours	first-aid post
poster	to post
potable	drinkable; drinking (water)
poterie f	pottery
poudre f	powder
pour	for
pourboire m	tip
pourquoi	why
pousser	to push
poussette f	push chair
premier(-ière)	first
premiers secours	first aid
prendre	to take; to get; to catch
prénom m	first name
près de	near (to)
préservatif m	condom
pressing m	dry cleaner's
prêt(e)	ready
prêt-à-porter m	off-the-peg clothes

French	English
prévision f	forecast
prière de...	please...
principal(e) m	main
printemps m	spring
priorité f	right of way
priorité à droite	give way to traffic from right
privé(e)	private
prix m	price; prize
à prix réduit	cut-price
prix d'entrée	admission fee
problème m	problem
prochain(e)	next
proche	close (near)
produits mpl	produce; product
profond(e)	deep
promotionnel(le)	on offer
propriétaire m/f	owner
propriété f	property
provisoire	temporary
public m	audience
pull(over) m	sweater
PV m	parking ticket

Q

French	English
quai m	platform
quand	when
quart m	quarter
quartier m	neighbourhood; district
que	that; than; what
qu'est-ce que c'est?	whom; what what is it?
quel(le)	which; what
quelque	some
quelque chose	something
queue: faire la queue	to queue (up)
qui	who; which

R

French	English
rabais m	reduction
radiographie f	X-ray
rafraîchissements mpl	refreshments
rage f	rabies
ralentir	to slow down
randonnée f	hike
randonnée à cheval	pony-trekking
rappel m	reminder (on signs)
rapide m	express train
raquette f	racket; bat; snowshoe
rasoir m	razor
RATP f	Paris transport authority
RC	ground floor
récepteur m	receiver (of phone)

French – English

French – English

réception f	reception; check-in	renseignements mpl	information	retard m	delay
recette f	recipe	réparations fpl	repairs	retour m	return
réchaud de camping m	camping stove	repas m	meal	retourner	to go back
réclamation f	complaint	repasser	to iron	retrait m	withdrawal; collection
reçu m	receipt	répondre (a)	to reply; to answer	retrait d'espèces	cash withdrawal
réduction f	reduction; discount; concession	réponse f	answer; reply	retraité(e)	retired; old-age pensioner
		représentation f	performance	réveil m	alarm clock
régime m	diet	requis(e)	required	rez-de-chaussée m	ground floor
région f	region	RER m	high-speed Paris commuter train	rhume m	cold (illness)
reine f	queen			rhume des foins	hay fever
relais routier m	roadside restaurant	réservation f	reservation; booking	rien	nothing
				rien à déclarer	nothing to declare
remède m	remedy	réserve naturelle f	nature reserve	rivière f	river
remplir	to fill (up); to fill in/out			RN	trunk road
rencontrer	to meet	réservé(e)	reserved	roi m	king
rendez-vous m	date; appointment	restoroute m	roadside or motorway restaurant	roman(e)	Romanesque

French	English
rond(e)	round
rond-point m	roundabout
rose	pink
rose f	rose
rôtisserie f	steakhouse; roast meat counter
roue f	wheel
roue de secours f	spare wheel
rouge	red
rougeur f	rash (skin)
route f	road; route
route barrée f	road closed
Royaume-Uni m	United Kingdom
rue f	street
rue sans issue f	no through road
ruelle f	lane; alley
russe	Russian

S

French	English
sable m	sand
sables mouvants	quicksand
sac m	sack; bag
sac à dos	backpack
sac à main	handbag
sac de couchage	sleeping bag
saison f	season
basse saison f	low season
de saison	in season
haute saison f	high season
salle f	lounge (airport); hall; ward (hospital)
salle à manger f	dining room
salle d'attente f	waiting room
salle de bains f	bathroom
salon m	sitting room; lounge
salon de beauté	beauty salon
samedi m	Saturday
SAMU m	emergency services
sang m	blood
sans	without
sans alcool	alcohol-free
sans issue	no through road
santé f	health
sapeurs-pompiers mpl	fire brigade
sauf	except (for)
savoir	(to know) (be aware of)
savoir faire quelque chose	to know how to do sth
savon m	soap
scène f	stage
sec (sèche)	dry; dried (fruit, beans, etc.)

French – English

French – English

sèche-cheveux m	hairdryer	
second(e)	second (in sequence)	
seconde f	second (in time)	
secours m	help	
au secours!	help!	
sécurité f	security; safety	
séjour m	stay; visit	
sel m	salt	
self m	self-service restaurant	
semaine f	week	
sens m	meaning; direction	
sens interdit	no entry	
sens unique	one-way street	
septembre m	September	
seringue f	syringe	
serrure f	lock	
servez-vous	help yourself	

service m	service; service charge; favour	
service compris	service included	
service d'urgences	emergency services	
serviette f	towel; briefcase	
serviette hygiénique	sanitary towel	
seulement	only	
sexe m	sex	
shampooing m	shampoo	
short m	shorts	
si	if; yes (to negative question)	
siècle m	century	
siège m	seat; head office	
signer	to sign	
situé(e)	located	
ski m	ski; skiing	
ski de piste	downhill skiing	

ski de randonnée/fond	cross-country skiing	
ski nautique	water-skiing	
SNCB f	Belgian Railways	
SNCF f	French Railways company	
société f	society	
sœur f	sister	
soie f	silk	
soif f	thirst	
avoir soif	to be thirsty	
soin m	care	
soins du visage	facial	
soir m	evening	
soirée f	evening; party	
soldes mpl	sales	
soleil m	sun; sunshine	
somnifère m	sleeping pill	
sorte f	kind (sort, type)	

French	English
sortie f	exit
sortie de secours	emergency exit
sortie interdite	no exit
sortir	to go out (leave)
souper m	supper
sourd(e)	deaf
sous	underneath; under
sous-sol m	basement
sous-titres mpl	subtitles
souterrain(e)	underground
souvent	often
sparadrap m	sticking plaster
spectacle m	show (in theatre); entertainment
sport m	sport
sports nautiques m	water-sports
stade m	stadium
stage m	course
station f	station (metro); resort
station balnéaire	seaside resort
station de taxis	taxi rank
station-service	service station
station thermale	spa
stationnement m	parking
sud m	south
suisse	Swiss
Suisse f	Switzerland
suivre	to follow
supermarché m	supermarket
supplément m	extra charge
supplémentaire	extra
sur	on; onto; on top of; upon
sur place	on the spot
sûr	safe; sure
surf m	surfing
faire du surf	to surf
surf des neiges	snowboarding
syndicat d'initiative m	tourist office

T

French	English
tabac m	tobacco; tobacconist's
table f	table
tableau m	painting; picture; board
taille f	size (of clothes); waist
taille unique	one size
grande taille	outsize (clothes)
tard	late
tarif m	price-list; rate; tarif
tasse f	cup; mug
taux m	rate

French – English

French – English

French	English
taux de change	exchange rate
taxe f	duty; tax (on goods)
taxi m	cab (taxi)
télé f	TV
télécabine f	gondola lift
télécarte f	phonecard
téléphérique m	cable-car
téléphone m	telephone
téléphone portable	mobile phone
téléphoner (à)	to phone
télésiège m	chair-lift
télévision f	television
temps m	weather; time
tenir	to hold; to keep
tension f	voltage; blood pressure
tente f	tent
tenue f	clothes; dress
tenue de soirée	evening dress

French	English
terrain m	ground; land; pitch; course
terrasse f	terrace
tête f	head
TGV m	high-speed train
thé m	tea
thé au lait	tea with milk
thé nature	black tea
théâtre m	theatre
ticket m	ticket (bus, cinema, museum)
ticket de caisse	receipt
timbre m	stamp
tirer	to pull
tirez	pull
toilettes f pl	toilet(s); washroom
tonalité f	dialling tone
tôt	early
total m	total (amount)

French	English
toucher	to touch
toujours	always; still; forever
tour f	tower
tour m	trip; walk; ride
tourisme m	sightseeing
tourner	to turn
tous	everyone; all
tous les jours	daily
tousser	to cough
tout	everything
tout/toute/toutes/tous	all
tout à l'heure	in a while
tout compris	all inclusive
tout de suite	straight away
tout droit	straight ahead
tout le monde	everyone
toutes directions	all routes
toux f	cough

French	English
tradition *f*	custom (*tradition*)
traduction *f*	translation
train *m*	train
tranche *f*	slice
tranquille	quiet (*place*)
travail *m*	work
travailler	to work (*person*)
travaux *mpl*	road works; alterations (*building*)
travers: à travers	through; to cross (*road, sea*)
tremplin de ski *m*	ski jump
très	very; much
trop	too; too much
trottoir *m*	pavement; sidewalk
trou *m*	hole

French	English
trousse de premiers secours *f*	first aid kit
TVA *f*	VAT
typique	typical

U

French	English
UE *f*	EU
un(e)	one; a; an
l'un ou l'autre	either one
université *f*	university
urgence *f*	urgency; emergency
urgences	accident and emergency department
usine *f*	factory
utiliser	to use

V

French	English
vacances *fpl*	holiday(s)
en vacances	on holiday
grandes vacances	summer holiday(s)
vaccin *m*	vaccination
vache *f*	cow
valable	valid (*ticket, licence, etc.*)
valeur *f*	value
valise *f*	suitcase
vallée *f*	valley
valoir	to be worth
ça vaut...	it's worth...
végétal(e)	vegetable
végétalien(ne)	vegan
végétarien(ne)	vegetarian
véhicule *m*	vehicle
véhicules lents	slow vehicles
vélo *m*	bike
vendre	to sell
à vendre	for sale
vendredi *m*	Friday

French – English

French – English

vénéneux	poisonous	**virage** m	bend; corner	**voisin(e)** m/f	neighbour
venir	to come	**visage** m	face	**voiture** f	car; coach (of train)
vent m	wind	**visite** f	visit; consultation (of doctor)	**vol** m	flight; theft
vente f	sale	**visite guidée**	guided tour	**vol intérieur**	domestic flight
verglas m	black ice	**visiteur (-euse)** m/f	visitor	**volonté:**	
verre m	glass			**à volonté**	as much as you like
verres de contact	contact lenses	**vite**	quickly; fast	**voyageur (-euse)** m/f	traveller
		vitesse f	gear (of car); speed	**VTT** m	mountain bike
vers	toward(s); about	**vitesse limitée à...**	speed limit...	**vue** f	view; sight
vestiaire m	cloakroom			**W**	
vêtements mpl	clothes	**vivre**	to live	**w-c** mpl	toilet(s);
vétérinaire m/f	vet	**voici**	here is/are	**wagon-couchettes** m	washroom; sleeping car
veuillez...	please...	**voie** f	lane (of road); line; track		
via	by (via)	**voilà**	there you are	**wagon-restaurant** m	dining car
viande f	meat	**voile** f	sail; sailing		
vieux (vieille)	old	**voilier** m	sailing boat		
vigne f	vine; vineyard	**voir**	to see		
vignoble m	vineyard				
village m	village				
ville f	town; city				
vin m	wine				

Y

yaourt *m* — yoghurt
yaourt nature — plain yoghurt
yeux *mpl* — eyes
youyou *m* — dinghy

Z

zéro *m* — zero
zone *f* — zone
zone piétonne — pedestrian area
zoo *m* — zoo

Further titles in Collins' phrasebook range
Collins Gem Phrasebook

Also available as **Phrasebook CD Pack**
Other titles in the series

Arabic	Greek	Polish
Cantonese	Italian	Portuguese
Croatian	Japanese	Russian
Czech	Korean	Spanish
Dutch	Latin American	Thai
French	Spanish	Turkish
German	Mandarin	Vietnamese

Collins Phrasebook & Dictionary

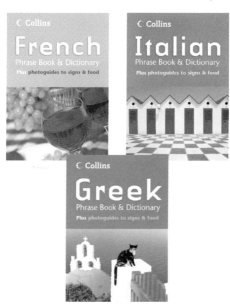

Also available as **Phrasebook CD Pack**
Other titles in the series
German Japanese Portuguese Spanish

Collins Easy: Photo Phrasebook

Also available as
**Phrasebook
CD Pack**

**Other titles
in the series**
Easy French
Easy Greek
Easy Italian

To order any of these titles, please telephone
0870 787 1732. For further information about all
Collins books, visit our website: www.collins.co.uk